My Brother, My Rapist

CHILD OF A **REBEL** SOLDIER

CHARLESETTA KOLB

ISBN: 978-1539952374

ONE

MY NAME IS CHARLESETTA DARLENE KOLB. I was born in Monrovia, the capital city of Liberia, on February 10, 1981. I was the youngest child of Charles Dean, called J.D., and Onike Thomas. My parents never married one another, so my older brother, sister, and I were known throughout our hometown as bastard children.

When I was very young, I lost my sister. I never got the chance to know her. My brother Todenny and I also never got to know our father as children; he left for the United States when I was only two days old. We lived in a family compound owned by my maternal grandfather; my mother waited until my grandfather was out, broke into his safe, and gave the money to my father to finance his trip to America.

My father promised to come back for us as soon as he had established himself in the United States. Though I never knew him, I looked forward to his return with excitement. When he came back, my mother said we would be a family again. We would move to America, live in a big house, and attend a great school.

That never happened. As soon as my father arrived in the United States, just days after he had promised my mother he would return, he met an African American woman. They married and had a child later the same year.

My mother, Onike, had no idea what he had done. My father still called her and promised that he would soon be back to get her. He promised to send money soon. But all those years he was in the United States, he never sent a dime.

As we were to find out later, he eventually divorced his son's mother. However, he still couldn't keep his promise to my mother. Soon after the divorce, he married a white woman named Kim and had another baby with her. My paternal grandfather, Charles Dean I, knew that my father had married Kim and had a baby girl, but he kept it a secret from my mother.

In the beginning my mother patiently waited for her love, but after several years, she reached her breaking point. With no options and no money coming in from my father, she showed up at my father's parents' door with a friend and demanded financial support. As soon as they came through the doorway, she saw a picture of my father and Kim.

I'm not close with my mother. She was hard and uncaring when I was a small child; she showed no interest in spending time with me, pushing me away even when I cried. But heartless as she was, I imagine that whatever was left of her heart shattered when she saw the photo of my father with another woman. She got a friend to take her downtown to the telecommunication office and dialed the phone angrily.

"Hello, can I speak to J.D.?"

A woman's voice answered the phone. "This is his wife, Kim. He's not home. Can I take a message?"

"Yes," my mother answered hesitantly. "Please tell J.D. his sister Onike Thomas called from Africa." She hung up the phone and stared at the receiver.

In West Africa, it is said that Americans are quick to kill their husband or wife when they are unfaithful. As much as she hated my father at that moment, my mother didn't want him to die at another woman's hand.

When she returned home, she was bitter. My father called every day, but she never returned his calls. His letters piled up in the mailbox unread. Finally, he must have known there was no way he could get through to her from across the ocean. He made the trip home to Liberia.

When he got to the home where we lived with my mother and maternal grandparents, she wasn't home. He decided to wait in her room. Since she had found out about my father, she had taken to staying out late in town, drinking with friends. As he grew angry and worried, my grandmother cooked a hot meal and brought up a plate, trying uncomfortably to make him feel at home.

My mother returned home the next morning to see my father sleeping in her bed. My brother and I peered around the doorway, watching to see what would happen. I watched as rage burned across her face. She jumped toward him, swinging her fists, but he skillfully caught her wrist. She reached down, pulled her sweetie slipper off of her foot, and slammed it upward into his face, breaking his nose. The eighteen stitches he had to get at the hospital that morning spelled the end of their romance.

The next day, my mother announced that she was separating Todenny and I. She wouldn't explain why. She hauled Todenny outside and took him to my grandfather Dean's; they would raise him and my mother would keep me. Todenny was my best friend; even as a child I knew he was the only one, besides my grandmother, that I could trust. As he was led off down the road, he turned to look toward me, but she pulled at his arm and his head snapped forward. As he disappeared down the road, tears blurred my eyes. My nightmare had begun.

TWO

IN OUR FAMILY COMPOUND, the first big house belonged to my grandmother. The second big house belonged to Auntie Buwa. There were two small houses belonging to my grandmother's siblings. Then there was a small home that my grandfather had built for us, but which my mother rented out for extra money. The homes were built close to one another, and we shared one bedroom in the main house. Although I missed Todenny terribly, I was comforted by the feeling of being surrounded by family, especially my grandmother.

My mother began to disappear for days on end, leaving me with my grandmother to go out with her friends. When she came home, her breath smelled of alcohol and her face looked haggard and worn. I dreaded the times when she came home. When she was drunk, she would fight anyone who she felt was looking at her the wrong way. She screamed at my grandmother as the old woman cried.

My mother had been spoiled from a young age; she had never worked a day in her life. She had a reputation for being spoiled and selfish. From a young age, her friends had called her B.G.—short for "bad girl." She relished the nickname, saying that it defined her. And it did. She would watch me fight till she saw blood. She stole my grandfather's money from his safe; she stole gas cards from his wallet and sold them for cash or alcohol. She would invite her friends, a useless bunch, to get drunk with the stolen money.

She used men for their money, staying at their homes and stealing their wallets. All Onike's children had two fathers, she would say, laughing; she would tell her lovers they were our fathers, and then they would pay child support directly to her.

She had several friends on the police force, and she would have them lock her up in jail. Her best friend would call Grandfather and tell him that my mother had hit someone in the head with a beer bottle or beaten a man in the street. He would believe them, as he knew his daughter was violent, and would bail her out of jail. As soon as the money came in, she and the policemen would split it.

When my grandfather passed away, it was very hard on my mother. She had always been a daddy's girl. Aside from being there to bail her out, he doted on her, forgiving her time and again for the theft and trouble. She had truly loved him. During his burial, she threw herself into the grave and screamed at the family to bury her with him. I clutched at my grandmother's hand in horror as I watched her fight off her family members; it took six men to eventually pull her out of the grave. She wore black for several years after his death in memory.

● ● ●

As much as she missed my grandfather, however, Onike didn't change her lifestyle. Without an easy source of money, she simply had to become a more intelligent criminal. One of her schemes was to rent out a fictional property. She collected the checks in advance, then failed to produce the rental property on move-in day. Unsurprisingly, the renters called the police, who arrested my mother. My grandmother now had to take on the responsibility of bailing my mother out of trouble. Grandmother paid the renters back their money to keep Onike out of jail.

Not a day went by without my mother getting drunk or getting into trouble. My grandmother begged her to stay home, but I couldn't wait for her to leave so I could play with my friends in peace. As I went to bed each night, I would pray that she wouldn't come back home. Whenever she did, she would wake me out of my sleep and demand that I squeeze her toes, scratch her back, or run my fingers through her hair until she fell asleep. If I fell asleep before she did, she would kick me hard and force me to sit up and continue.

After keeping me up all night, she would wake me up early and force me to buy the ingredients for whatever food she wanted to eat that day. I would help her cook and then she would take a long bath. While all my friends started school, my mother left me home alone all day with a list of chores. The lists were long and impossible to get through, but if I didn't complete them all, she would beat me in the chest with a metal spoon.

As her alcoholism grew worse, my mother began to terrorize the neighborhood as well. Cousins and aunts would flee my grandmother's home when they heard her coming. Even her own mother's patience began to wear thin.

Finally, my mother met a man named Steve. He married her and moved her away from the family compound. Grandmother was delighted; Steve was gentle, polite, and responsible. He had great job in accounting, and his family owned a lot of property. He was also very much in love with my mother and took good care of us in his new home.

As the years passed, my mother and Steve had four children. My mother took me out of school and I remained home to take care of my three brothers and sister. This struck me as incredibly unfair. While Steve's two older children attended one of the best schools in Africa, my mother would not let me attend any school. Instead, I rose early in the morning to fetch bathwater for Steve before he left for work. I walked my siblings to school and came back to clean the house, fetch water, and go to the market. At three o'clock, I would return to school to pick up my siblings. Meanwhile, my mother loafed around with her friends. She would make sure to come home one hour before Steve returned from work so that we could get dinner on the table; he would think that she had done the cleaning and cooking herself while I was at school. I helped bitterly, knowing that my siblings would get the best part of the meal. I would get the leftover scraps not fit for a dog. I felt like Cinderella in my own home.

Finally, I worked up the courage to ask my mother why I could not go to school with my sister and brother. She glared at me and responded, "Dirt like you can't go to school with decent children. Don't you know I found you in the trash can?"

I stared at her, wide-eyed, as her face twisted into a sneer. "Now get your ass in the house and clean the bathroom until I see my face shine on the floor, since I guess you've got nothing to do but question me."

As I scrubbed the bathroom sink, my rage grew. It was unfair that I was missing out on life to clean toilets and fetch water while my mother got all the credit. That night, I pulled Steve aside and whispered that I was not in school. He grew upset with my mother, and I could hear them arguing behind their bedroom door late into the night.

The next morning, I took my siblings to school. Steve hadn't said anything to me about school, so I returned home reluctantly to face my mother. Without a word, she muscled me into the bathroom, a razor clutched in her hand. I sobbed in surprise as she shaved my head with satisfaction. Then she pulled me outside, grabbing a hot pepper and crushing it between her fingers along the way. She smeared the seeds into my eyes, then reached down my pants and pressed her fingers against the sensitive skin of my vagina. Then she told me to stand in the sun. As I stood in the yard, crying in pain and humiliation, she growled that this was my punishment for talking to her husband behind her back.

After that time, it seemed her personal mission was to do everything she could to make me unattractive. The shaved head was not enough; she began to wake me in the middle of the night to beat my breasts with a metal spoon. When I cried out that it felt like I was going to die, she hissed that she was trying to help me; my breasts would just make me frisky if she didn't take care of them.

I never understood why Steve stayed with my mother. They rarely went out together. Several times, when they had gone out together at night, they got into such violent fights that my mother tore Steve's clothes off. She would embarrass him with her screams until he ran away from her; often their nights out would end with him returning home to change his clothes.

Steve's family saw all this. They knew my mother's reputation and how she treated Steve and her children. They begged him to leave her; they didn't like her. However, one person did—Jim, Steve's brother. One morning I spied the two of them, after Steve had gone to work, kissing in the bedroom.

● ● ●

Several months after she had shaved my head, my father's father sent a messenger with the news that Todenny was dead. As soon as she found out about my brother's death, Onike went straight to my father's house and attacked him for murdering Todenny. The whole neighborhood came out to watch as Onike screamed in the street; her dead son was wrapped up in a blanket in the house. It took an agonizingly long time for her to calm down and give instructions on how she wanted Todenny to be buried.

As my brother's body was lowered into the ground, my world had ended.

• • •

I didn't think it was possible, but after my brother's death, Onike's hatred toward me became even stronger. She would turn to me, her eyes flashing in anger, and say that I should have been the one to die. "You're not my daughter," she spat. "You're ugly and no one cares about you. You will never go anywhere in life. You'll be a slave to your siblings; all your life you'll be begging them for food and clothing." She would say these evil things in front of my siblings. She would instruct them to beat me and tell me not to raise my hand.

As much as I hated Onike, I was a child. I craved her attention; I craved love from anyone. I saw how she held the hands of my brothers and sister and tried to convince her to love me, to hold me. But if I acted like I was happy when my mother was around, she would give me a look that made the hair on my arms stand up.

My first criminal act for my mother was stealing a chicken from our neighbors and selling it downtown so she could use the money to get drunk. After the success of this first endeavor, she began demanding that I steal more and more to feed her addiction. When the chickens ran out, I began stealing our neighbors' clothes and anything of value. When Steve allowed a family friend to rent out the extra bedroom, she broke into the renter's room, stole his boom box, and made me sell it downtown.

None of this earned me my mother's love. It only earned me more beatings; Onike split my head open with a beer bottle when I took too long selling the stolen goods.

THREE

IN 1989, LIBERIA ERUPTED in civil war. My family and I had to run for our lives. That's when Onike and Steve separated. When it was safe to return, my mother moved us back to my grandmother's home in the family compound.

Our family depended on Auntie Buwa Gibson for financial help, but she was married to the Speaker of the House, so they always had extra money to give. Life was good; I felt the warmth of my grandmother's love and enjoyed being surrounded by aunts and cousins.

When I was nine years old, in 1990, the war started again. Because of our uncle's work, we were considered a political family and thus a target for the rebels. When the rebels attacked Monrovia, Auntie Buwa and her children took my grandmother and ran away to Ghana. The rest of the family didn't have the financial means to leave the country. My mother, my siblings, and I ran to the nearest town that hadn't been taken by rebels.

We had lost everything we owned. Soldiers roamed the streets, shooting innocent people, breaking into homes, and burning down everything in their path. We had seen them slaughter children and rip babies out of pregnant women.

Finally, a cease-fire was declared, and we were able to return home. Our compound had been raided, everything stolen, but it had not been burned. We had nothing left but the clothes on our back, but we were happy to be alive. We joyously reunited with my uncle and his family there, camping out uneasily in one house.

One morning, just as we were beginning to settle in again, we awoke to the sound of gunfire. We heard the soldiers barking orders at our neighbors, my family members. We could hear familiar voices crying out, "Please don't kill us—take everything we have, but please don't kill my family."

Multiple AK-47 shots rang out. We knew the entire household was dead. Crouching in the corner, my younger sister began to cry. My mother reached over and clamped her hand over my sister's mouth. If the soldiers heard her, our entire family was next, as well as my uncle and his family, who lay on the floor next to us in silence.

We remained in that room for three days without food. Luckily, we had a reserve of water. We passed around a bucket as a toilet; the smell soon began to make me sick. As I grew progressively more ill, I lost the ability to speak or walk. I lay on the floor, my legs weak and heavy. I had begun to soil my pants constantly and could not control my bladder; I was pumping out nothing but water. The adults whispered that I had cholera, but there was no way to get to a doctor.

On the fourth day, my uncle said that the time had come for us to leave. My mother crawled outside and whispered back to us that there were no soldiers in sight. She crossed the room again and put me onto her back, took my youngest siblings by the hand, and nodded toward the door.

The rest of my family rose silently and stole out into the street, leaving all their belongings behind. We made our way silently toward the trees, leaping over dead bodies as we ran. Though we knew our family members lay among them, there was no time to see which of the bodies belonged to us.

I clutched weakly at my mother's shoulders and closed my eyes. It was the first time I had ever felt close to her.

● ● ●

We finally made it to our destination, which was my grandmother's sister's house in rack culture. The rebels had not yet taken over that part of town, and the house was large, so all of my family members had made their way there. My relief faded, however, when my mother told my family that I had cholera. They told my mother that I couldn't stay in the house. She carried me outside and laid me down by the bathroom. It was a hole in the ground topped with a crude wooden structure and a swing door, and it didn't flush. As she walked away, I cried out, the smell of the waste making me feel even sicker. She didn't turn around.

The hours dragged by slowly and then blurred together, turning into weeks. I would watch as family members passed me on their way to the toilet; they were afraid to touch me. My mother came each day to lay water and a piece of bread beside me, but with the smell and the pain ripping through my stomach, I could barely eat it. I slept and struggled to pour water into my parched lips while lying in my own waste. My eyes began to sink back into my head, and my family members could count every bone in my body. They told my mother that I wasn't going to make it, and she believed them.

After several weeks, she disappeared for a few days and returned with a native doctor. By some miracle of God, I was still alive. He quickly examined me, then cooked up some leaves in a pot and gave me cup of the mixture to drink. At night he returned and instructed me to drink more, then covered me with a blanket he had warmed over the boiling pot. He returned each day for a week, repeating the ritual. A few days later, I began to feel better. During his last visit, I found the strength to walk again.

I stayed outside for several more nights, as I wasn't completely well. One morning, my mother came outside to get me, telling me that Nigerian peacekeepers had succeeded in cooling down some of the fighting in our town. We returned to Lane Street slowly and painfully. I struggled to walk; my stomach was still distended, my feet swollen, and my bones protruded like those of a skeleton. I stared wide-eyed at the rubble around our old home. My family members leaned in over the wreckage, picking up whatever pieces they could from the ashes of their homes. My aunts and uncles doubled over in tears, crying over the lost members of our family.

That was my first experience with death.

FOUR

AFTER LIBERIA SETTLED DOWN, my mother became pregnant. Once my sister was born, she moved us away from the family compound. All six of us stayed in a cramped, dilapidated one-bedroom home.

You would think that after all we had been through in the war, something would have changed within my mother. She had seen family members die, had carried me on her back through the fighting, had almost lost me and then watched as I recovered and began my life again. But nothing in her attitude had evolved. She went out all day without a single word, leaving my siblings and I alone with nothing to eat. I didn't know what to do; I fed the baby water all day long as she cried. In the evenings, my mother returned home drunk. As soon as she fell asleep, I would pull out her breast so the baby could eat.

I grew so desperate that I asked our neighbors for help, and sometimes they took pity on us and gave us food. Most of the time we offered to work for the food, cleaning their home and yard. I worried all day about how to keep my brothers and sisters fed, and when Onike returned home drunk each night, my anger grew.

One day she returned with half a bag of rice. She called my siblings and I into the house and told us that she was going out of town to get some coal to sell wholesale.

She left for two weeks. My desperation grew; my sister screamed constantly. We had nothing to eat but rice and red oil. I began to overcook the rice, softening it as much as I could and gently spooning it into the baby's mouth. I tied her to my back while I cleaned the house and looked after my siblings. When my friends came to the door, looking to play, I turned them away in disappointment.

After Onike had been gone for several days, our neighbor brought over some soup for us to eat. My siblings yelped in joy. I laid the baby on the bed and put the bottle in her mouth so the other children and I could eat. After eating, happy and warm, we fell asleep.

The next morning, I awoke next to the baby. I tried to wake her to feed her, but she was still sound asleep, so I left her and went outside to get started with chores. Our neighbor called over to ask where my younger sister was, and I responded that she was still asleep and wouldn't wake up to eat. Curious, she went into the room to check on her. A moment later, she came back outside, a panicked look on her face, screaming that the baby was dead.

The whole neighborhood gathered in front of our door, asking for my mother. I simply shook my head, crying in confusion.

Onike came finally came home to a dead child. I wouldn't have thought it was possible for her hatred of me to grow, but it did. She greeted me with screams and accusations that I had killed my sister. My mother's abuse finally grew so unbearable that I ran away from home.

After I had hidden myself out in the neighborhood, though, I began to think. Who would take care of my siblings as Onike lay around the house drunk? I could not bear to return home, but I felt my stomach turn over with guilt and terror when I thought about what would happen to them. Finally, I asked a few neighborhood boys to run and tell my mother they had seen me. I knew she would send them back to catch me, and I would let them take me home. I knew there would be a serious punishment for running away, but I steeled myself. I could not leave my siblings alone.

FIVE

THE REBELS HADN'T FINISHED WITH LIBERIA, and they soon returned to take it over again. My second encounter with death came in 1995. At the time, I didn't know how to spell or write my own name, and certainly didn't know my birthday. So I couldn't have told you how old I was then, but looking back, I know I must have been ten years old.

With the reoccurrence of war, bad luck also revisited me. I had fallen so ill that I was unconscious and did not appear to be breathing anymore. Onike had once again given up all hope and thought I was dead.

As the rebels were approaching, there was no time for crying and no time to dig a grave to bury me. Thank God for that; I was very much alive. I'm not sure if Onike actually thought I was dead or if this was her opportunity to get rid of me. Perhaps she just didn't want to carry a sick child on her back again. Regardless of the reason, she wrapped me up and left me beside the house, where bullets were whizzing through the air. She gathered my siblings and fled, leaving me there alone. I lay on the ground, barely conscious but writhing with fever.

Soon afterward, a woman passed by, running beneath a hail of grenades and explosions to use the bathroom. Ducking aside for protection, she crawled around the side of the house where my mother had left me. As she squatted, she stared at what seemed to be a blanket moving slightly in the wind. She reached forward, moved aside the cover, and saw me lying there moaning. There was no time for her to think; she grabbed me and shouted for her husband to help carry me on his back. After we returned to her home, she started to nurse me back to life.

Once again I had escaped death; it just wasn't my time.

● ● ●

As I got well, I was confused. Who was the woman bringing me food and water, and where was my family?

"I believe they thought you were dead," the kind woman said, a look of sadness in her eyes. "We'll look for them after the gunfire stops. For now, you can rest and recover, and you can call me Auntie Judy."

Even at such a young age, I realized that she and her husband had risked their lives to save me. Again I had been sent a guardian angel. I was grateful and astonished; no one had ever risked anything for me, let alone a stranger. Recovering there, I felt a comfort I had never felt before in my life.

However, it was not to last for long. As they lived in a one-bedroom home, Judy and her husband slept in the bed, and I slept by the foot of the bed on the floor. Judy normally fell asleep very early; her husband came to bed very late, as he and the other men stay up listening for sounds of the rebels coming our way. Every night when he come to bed, he would climb over me in the dark and try to pry my legs apart.

I was confused. I squeezed my legs shut and he finally gave up. I thought maybe it was a mistake; maybe he thought I was his wife. But several nights passed, and every night he tried again. I knew that he wasn't going to give up. One night, I slipped out of the room and ran away.

As I ran through the darkness, I felt so ungrateful; I had never thanked Auntie Judy. I also had nowhere to go. I could not return to Lane Street; that side of town was now the head rebel checkpoint. I stole down the slipway in the other direction, hoping to see some of my family from my father's side. I didn't see anyone; my grandfather's house had been burned down. In place of the neighborhood were eerie piles of ashes. The only thing left standing was the church and school my grandfather had attended. With no other options in sight, I headed to Bushrod Island to hide from the soldiers.

The island lay across a bridge from the biggest marketplace in that part of town, called Down Water Said. It had formerly been a residential neighborhood; now it was full of the dead. I lay under a bridge in the dark, trying to sleep, terrified by every small sound in the brush.

In the morning I rose and scrounged around, looking for food. This became a daily ritual. I went for weeks without bathing or changing my dirty panties. Luckily I could drink the water that flowed across the island in streams, but I was too terrified to emerge from cover to bathe.

One day I decided to try my luck and cross the bridge to look for food and clothing in the marketplace. I made my way across the bridge quickly and quietly, but before I reached the other side, four young soldiers stepped out of the woods.

One pointed his gun at me and barked, "Come here."

My heart raced in panic. My body trembled violently, and tears welled in my eyes. "Please don't kill me," I begged.

The youngest yelled, "Shut up before I blow your brains out."

"Where are you going?" asked the first soldier.

Choking on tears, I stared at the ground. "I lost my family. They thought I was dead. They left me, and now I don't know where they are. I am trying to find food."

The soldiers looked at each other and had a rushed, quiet conversation.

Finally, the first soldier announced that he felt sorry for me, and I looked like one of his little sisters. He was going to keep me. He grabbed hold of my arm firmly and stalked off down the road, dragging me behind him.

SIX

THE SOLDIERS ESCORTED ME to their base station. Most of the bases we had were captured or abandoned government compounds, but in some cases they had been wealthy, secluded estates where government officials had lived before the soldiers had taken over. When we first moved into a compound, we had to secure it, ensuring no one would take it from us.

Some compounds were barely looted, still gorgeous and whole, while others were vandalized and in shambles nearly unrecognizable as the palaces they had once been. When we moved into a compound, we brought supplies—food, weapons, sandbags for cover. There were also times when we didn't have a compound or town to claim. That was when we would stay out in the bush, roughing it and taking turns on watch.

The soldier who had taken me under his wing introduced himself as we went inside. "Call me Baboon," he said, smiling slightly.

There were three other young girls at the station, he informed me; I would be staying with them. He showed me into their room and ordered them to help me draw water for a bath and find some clean clothes to wear.

Terrified as I was, it felt good to wash the weeks of filth off my skin. The dirt flaked off into the bath water as I scrubbed; then I took the coarse new clothes and wrapped them around my body. Afterward, the women brought me a plate of food. I was so full for the first time in a long time. I lay down afterward, warm and exhausted, and fell into a deep sleep.

After I had eaten and rested for three days, Baboon called me outside. Most of the soldiers from the base were lined up, practicing shooting. He gave me my first AK-47 and told me to empty it.

I looked at him in confusion. The gun was cold and hard in my hands; it was very heavy and difficult to hold. Seeing it made my heartbeat spike in intense fear. I didn't know what they expected me to do with it.

"Shoot until the gun is empty," he said, gesturing forward into the empty street. I pulled the trigger like I had seen the men in town do. The gun kicked backward, startling me. Gritting my teeth, I pulled the trigger again and shot until the gun was empty.

"Good," he said, satisfied. "You are now a soldier."

I looked around at the group. They were a ragged group of youngsters—some muscular teens with ripped clothing and blank looks on their faces, some just children with wiry arms and tiny legs. The youngest in the group was six. I looked for some sign of understanding but found only blank stares. All of their eyes were red. I suddenly felt a cold certainty that if I were to say no, or even hesitate, they would kill me.

At eleven years old, I had no choice but to enter the war.

● ● ●

As the days passed, I was assigned to watch at doors and gates while the older soldiers smashed their way through doors and windows. Soon, I graduated to breaking into stores, stealing anything and everything.

One afternoon, we broke into a home and discovered a family hiding.

As I watched uncertainly from the doorway, the six-year-old soldier marched into the room and opened fire on the father and son. Another soldier grabbed hold of a crying pregnant girl and slashed a knife into her stomach. I watched in horror as he ripped the unborn baby out of her, blood staining the floor as she screamed.

"Why did you do that? Why are you doing that?" I cried in horror, momentarily forgetting myself.

The six-year-old turned toward me viciously and kicked hard into my shin. "Shut up," he snarled, "or you will die with them."

I pressed my lips together hard and tried not to look toward the bodies on the floor. We took all their money, food, and valuable things. It was the first time I had seen anyone killed up close.

As the days passed, I became one of them. I put the unborn baby out of my mind; I couldn't ask any more questions if I was to survive. I was told to kill a man who was running through the checkpoint. I didn't know if he was an enemy or not, but I was told to shoot, so I did. I saw the man fall to the ground. Baboon approached me and said, "You are a real soldier now. You must act like one. If not, the enemy will kill you."

Instantly, the sinking feeling of guilt and horror that had been slowly churning up in my stomach disappeared. It was replaced with a fierce resolve. I remembered my cousin and neighbors lying dead outside their home. I felt a hot rush of anger. I was going to take my revenge; I was going to do what I had to do to survive. Either the enemies would take my life or I was going to die taking theirs.

The next weeks passed by in a blur of anger and fear. Baboon gave me a nickname, Iron Jacket. I'm not a large woman and I was even smaller then. A generous person would say I'm about five feet tall, but I take pride in being just four foot eleven. An iron jacket is a small, strong person, someone Shakespeare would describe as little but fierce. It was around this time that I became fully involved in the war.

Throughout the chaos, I was often lost in thoughts of my family and the death of my only brother. Some of the soldiers I was with had fallen into a trap and died. My heart felt as if it exploded in sadness when I watched Baboon die in the crossfire. I forgot my anger; I forgot any old ideas of what I should or shouldn't do. I didn't care anymore. It was do or die, and I had already escaped death twice; I was determined to stay alive no matter the cost. Everything I knew was pain and I was boiling with anger. My instincts ran only to survival. There was nothing I cared about more than living to see the next day. Most of the time, I felt almost numb—soulless and abandoned—to the horrors we saw every day.

This absence of feeling clung to me for years. I had been taken in by the soldiers when I was around ten years old, a child who could not reason or understand in the ways an adult can, despite how long I had been caring for myself thanks to my alcoholic and hateful mother.

When the peacekeepers called for a cease-fire, I was fourteen. On their orders, I ditched my gun and uniform. I walked out of the base and did not look back.

• • •

I went looking for my family at our old home, but the rooms were dark and empty. Out in the street, I ran into my mother's half sister, who took me in to help out in her food shop. The shop was in a large, open-air bazaar and I helped her sell and prepare food and cool water. I did not work for her for very long before I encountered someone I thought I would never see again.

As I emerged from the shop to wash the dishes that day, I heard someone yelling my name. I looked up in shock to see a girl running toward me, her face open and grinning excitedly.

"Don't you know me?" she asked. "I am your sister Eunice!"

After a moment, I recognized her, seeing in her face how she had grown over the past few years, and reached toward her. Overjoyed, we both burst into tears.

"Where is Mother?" I asked her.

"She's over there drinking," she responded, her face twisted into a grimace.

I ran toward my mother. I couldn't believe my family was alive; I had long ago accepted the fact that I would never see them again. I was even glad to see her. I tried to hug her, to touch her.

She raised her eyebrows and said, "Oh, Darlene, you're okay." Her voice was flat, uncaring. She took another swig from her bottle, eyeing me.

There was no crying; she didn't shed a single tear of happiness or relief that I was alive. *She didn't even miss me, I thought. My stomach dropped at the sight of the bottle in her hands and the blank look on her face as she stared down the dusty street, looking anywhere but at me.*

● ● ●

Soon after I had reunited with my family, my mother began abusing me again. For several days, I kept my mouth shut, hoping it would pass, wanting so badly to have security and a family again. But I soon realized that I had seen too much and survived too much to suffer abuse at the hands of my mother.

I set out on the road one morning and did not come back. I went looking for my paternal grandfather. When I finally found him near where his old house had stood, he told me that he was looking for me as well. My father wanted me to join him in the United States. I was overjoyed and asked him to come with me to let my mother know.

But when we told her the good news, she replied flatly, "Over my dead body. You're not going to the United States."

Stunned, I appealed to my aunts and uncles. I asked everyone in the house to help me. My family advised her to let me go; even her friends, the good-for-nothing alcoholics who hung about our home like parasites, told her it was a good idea. She refused to budge or even explain. My grandfather finally set off for home without me, and I sobbed as I watched his back recede down the front path. He returned the next day and the day after, begging my mother to release me into his care, but he got the same response.

Thus it happened that when I first came to America in 1995, my mother didn't know. I stole out of the house without asking her; I stayed at my grandfather's home as arrangements were hurriedly made. I boarded a plane, the blood rushing in my ears, both relieved and terrified that I had finally made my escape. I thought it was the end of my suffering.

SEVEN

I MET MY BIOLOGICAL FATHER, Charles Dean, after dreaming of being his little girl for fourteen years. When the dream finally came true, in 1995, it was bittersweet.

When I disembarked the flight, I found that my father was married to his third wife, Sia Dean. She was pregnant with his fifth, and ultimately last, child. I was introduced to my little brother Ceephas, my father's other child, as soon as I arrived.

My father and Sia lived in a one-bedroom townhouse. My grandfather and I slept in the room. My sister only came over on the weekend, but she and I got along very well. My father took me everywhere he went, and my grandpa and I went with him to play soccer on the weekend. For the first time in my life, I was actually enjoying my childhood.

My first school in America was Kennedy High School. I was placed in an ESL class. I was fourteen years old, entering high school, and I couldn't read or write my own name. While I felt anxiety that I was so far behind the other students, I enjoyed school.

Soon afterward, my father and stepmother bought a three-bedroom townhouse. My grandfather had one room; Charles, Sia, and Ceephas had one room; and I had my own room for the first time. We soon fell into a comfortable daily routine. My stepmother went to work early in the morning, my dad went to work at night, my grandfather stayed home to watch Ceephas, and I went off to school. Life was normal, and everybody was happy.

That is, until Sia began asking me questions about my father's alleged infidelity. My father stopped taking me places because Sia was bribing me to tell her where we went and the names of people my father took me see. Charles had a couple of women that he was cheating on Sia with. They began fighting almost every day, and our once-happy home became a battleground.

One day, Charles came in with his son Jermell, who struck me immediately as a lost soul. I had to share my room with him, which I hated. Even worse was the way Sia acted once he moved in. She would go to the store and buy juice and crunchy ice cream for Ceephas and my father, but nothing we wanted to eat. Jermell and I began to wait for my parents to go to bed, then drink and eat all the juice and ice cream. Jermell would drink Ceephas' juice and fill the bottle with water. So our stepmother Sia put a lock on the fridge and forced us to ask whenever we wanted to eat.

After some time, I reported my stepmother to the school. A social worker came out, saw the lock on the fridge, and told my stepmother to remove it. As soon as the social worker left, my stepmother went ballistic. She started beating me and screaming at me for telling on her at school.

This was too familiar. I screamed back at her, "You are nothing to me! You aren't my mother! Why are you beating me?" Her face flashed, and she caught my arm and pushed me down the stairs into the basement.

Suddenly, I was overcome by flashbacks. My mother's face taunted me in my memory, slapping me, pushing me down, telling me I was worthless. Searching desperately around the basement, hysterical, I grabbed a rope that lay along the wall and slung it over a ceiling beam. I tried to hang myself.

When my grandfather made his way down the stairs into the dark basement, my eyes were rolling back in my head. He shouted for Sia to call 911, and the ambulance took me to the hospital.

Once I was discharged, I was taken to a mental institution. The mental institution kept me for two weeks or thirty days.

EIGHT

WHEN I RETURNED, I found that I had lost everything I felt for my father. I began to realize his absences and his reluctance to get involved in our upbringing. I admit that I was no angel. I got in trouble around the house for things like stealing money from my dad for lunch or stealing my stepmother's makeup and clothes. But you can hardly blame me; the clothes she bought me were embarrassing. I'd go to school in matching Mickey Mouse outfits—as a teenager.

I also got in trouble for fighting at school. You wouldn't have expected it. I was one of the shy kids. I walked with my head down, and I didn't have any friends. I was always nervous to go to the cafeteria. It was where I most felt the pain of being an outsider; it was where everyone else sat with their ready-made friend groups, and I sat alone. It was also the place where I was targeted.

A tall African American girl known throughout the school as a bully had chosen me as her victim. She pushed me into my locker whenever she walked by, made fun of my clothes loudly in the hallway, and sneered that

I was an "African booty scratcher." I reported her to the principal and my parents, but she continued to pick on me.

One day in the hallway, I'd had enough. As she walked by, barking out insults, I decided to show her the true definition of an African booty scratcher. I beat the shit out of that girl. I was suspended from school for two weeks, but it was worth it. On the day I returned, the tall girl's friends sat down next to me at the lunch table—and suddenly, I had friends.

NINE

I DIDN'T KNOW IT when I woke up that day, but Ceephas' first birthday was the day that would change my life. It was a birthday to remember for a one-year-old. There was a limousine, a DJ, and plenty of food and drinks—even alcohol. I was in a jealous fury from the moment the guests started rolling in.

All my life, I never had a birthday party, and here they were paying for a limousine for a baby who wouldn't even remember it. I felt so angry I could have killed them—and then they had the nerve to tell me to hold Ceephas in my lap for his limousine ride. It felt like my stepmother was rubbing salt in my wounds. I didn't understand why he couldn't sit on his own if he was old enough to have a birthday party like that. I didn't want to go on the limousine ride. People could see how angry I was. Just as it was beginning to dampen the mood of the party, my Uncle Eric's wife pulled me aside and asked me not to be angry. For Ceephas' sake, I began to pretend to be having fun.

As the party wore on, I actually did start to have fun. It was incredible.

The home was filled with friends and family dancing, drinking, talking, and laughing. When the last guest had left, my parents and grandfather went to their rooms and told Jermell and I to go to the room we shared.

About half an hour after we settled into our beds, Jermell said he was going to go get something to drink. When he came back up, he had two bottles filled with red liquid. He handed me one and he drank the other. The last thing I remember is the sweet taste of the liquid.

When I woke up the next morning, light streaming in the window, I felt strange. When I lifted the covers, I saw blood all over my sheets and staining through my underwear. I didn't mention anything about the feeling to my stepmother. I just assumed it was my period—until seven months later.

● ● ●

"You're pregnant," Uncle Eric's wife said to me. We were at a party in their home, seated at the kitchen table.

I looked at her and shook my head, laughing. I thought she was joking around. Yes, I'd gained weight since the last time I saw her. Was this her way of calling me fat?

Before I could stop her, she went over to my father and told him that I was pregnant. I rose from the table, protesting. "You're crazy!"

My father looked over at me, realization spreading across his face. She was a nurse, and it was clear that he didn't second-guess any diagnosis she gave. As we drove home from the party, my father said, "You're not going to school tomorrow. You're going to the doctor."

The next morning, I lay in bed thinking about what the day would have in store for me. My father took me to the hospital. They did their pregnancy test. After a few moments, the doctor came out and told me that it was positive.

I was pregnant.

My father drew his breath in sharply. "We need to remove it."

"No," the doctor said. "That would be murder. Your daughter is about seven and a half months pregnant."

I stopped breathing. After I had finally caught my breath, I looked up at my father. The look on his face was something I still can't explain.

How had this happened? My mind raced. I didn't have a boyfriend; apart from school, I didn't go anywhere without my parents. *How am I pregnant?*

My father asked me in the car, his voice shaking. I told him I didn't know. When we returned home, we told my grandfather. He asked me how, and I gave the same answer: I didn't know.

When my stepmother came home and found out the news, she asked me to go for a drive. "Think," she urged me, gripping the wheel. I stared out the window at the homes racing by, the neat lawns. I thought as hard as I could. Suddenly, I remembered something. Seven months ago, the blood on my sheets, the strange feeling and my lack of memory of the night after I'd finished my drink.

And then I knew.

I was raped by my half brother.

The words tumbled out of my mouth. I told her about the red drink that Jermell had given me, the strange feeling I had the next morning, the blood stains in my underwear. I told her that he had raped me. Her face froze, and then a strange expression came across it. I fidgeted in my seat, shoulders hunched, awaiting a response. When it came, it was unexpected.

"You're lucky you didn't say that your father did that to you. He would have killed you."

I stared at her. What was she talking about? I had just told her my half brother had raped me. I didn't understand why she would suggest that I could have said my father did it. Nothing she said made any sense.

When we got home, my stepmother told me to tell my father and grandfather what I had told her. I told them that Jermell had raped me. When Jermell came home from school, they questioned him. Jermell swore up and down that he would never do anything like that. I was a pathological liar, he said; he swore on his mother that I was lying. They believed him.

My father turned and said, "Go get your stuff. You're moving to the basement."

My basement imprisonment began. I wasn't allowed to sit upstairs and talk with anyone, watch television, or eat unless they were home.

My stomach grew, as did my depression. Feeling I had no options and embarrassed by my swelling size, I dropped out of school. I listened from the basement as the door slammed, listened to the sounds of my father leaving the house to cheat on my stepmother after she left for work.

My grandfather allowed me to venture upstairs to eat and watch television. I would sit upstairs all day, staring blankly at the screen, and run back to the basement as soon as I heard the garage door open. I shivered in the dark while Jermell and the rest of my family laughed around the dinner table.

One day, I decided I couldn't take it anymore. I rose from my bed, grabbed my father's free weights, and slammed them into my stomach. I was going to kill my baby. I slammed the weights into my swollen stomach over and over again, doing everything I could to kill the problem growing in my stomach.

Nothing worked. I carried the baby full term.

TEN

SIA CEEDAH DEAN WAS BORN on July 17, 1997, in Fairview Hospital in Richfield, Minnesota. Before the birth of my baby, my parents and I had decided to put her up for adoption. We had agreed that I would not see the baby, but for some reason, after my parents went home to clean up, a nurse brought the baby into my room and asked if I would like to feed her.

"No," I answered.

"Are you scared?" the nurse asked gently. "Try holding her. She's beautiful."

I took the baby gingerly into my arms. As I stared down at her tiny face, she wrapped her finger around mine, and I felt something I had never felt before. I started to cry—and believe it or not, the baby smiled. I knew right then I was going to keep her.

When the nurse came back in to check on us, she saw me playing with the baby and smiled. She sat down on the edge of the bed.

"I know you're young, but you carried the baby and you had her. You did a great job. You don't need to give your baby up for adoption if you don't want to. There is a lot of support out there for teenage mothers," she said.

I was still doubtful; the idea of life with a baby was terrifying. "You don't understand how this baby was conceived. She's my half brother's baby. He raped me. My family hates me because of it. I don't know if I can support her."

"What your brother did was wrong, but that baby is innocent. She deserves to know her mother." She looked at me kindly. "Will you keep your baby?"

Tears filled my eyes again. "Yes."

She leaned in, as though to give me a big hug, but suddenly my parents were walking in, so she excused herself from the room.

● ● ●

At this point we didn't have any adaption parents waiting to take the baby. I drew in my breath and announced that I wanted to take her home, and to my surprise, my parents agreed. We named her on the way home.

The first week home with Sia was very depressing. I realized suddenly what I had given up by having her; she was like a constant memory of how I had been beaten down in the past. Every time I looked at her, I began to cry. There were a few times that I pulled a pillow over her face, hoping that she would die. Each time, she kicked her hands and feet, and I took the pillow away and cried.

I didn't have a job. I didn't know anyone. I didn't have anywhere to go. I was sixteen years old, stuck in a home full of family members who despised me, saddled with a baby. I had no future; I didn't even know how to read or write. Here I was, back in the same house, playing brother and sister with the man who had raped me.

Each morning, I woke up to see Jermell going to school, acting like he had done nothing wrong. I sat in the basement and fantasized about how to kill him.

I knew damn well what he had done, and my parents knew; I knew they were ashamed. They claimed that they had had a blood test done at the hospital that proved Jermell was not the father. I knew they were lying. But later that week, when I was called in for another questioning by the Richfield Police Department, I told the detective that somebody had else raped me in the bathroom so the report I had made against Jermell would be dropped. I had to do anything I could to avoid the worst fate of all—returning to Africa.

I didn't get much help from my family; I was told I had to do it alone. My stepmother did show me what to do here and there when I asked for help. One day, I did walk in on my father playing with the baby and calling her Turkey. I guess he thought he was being a grandfather.

ELEVEN

A MONTH AFTER I RETURNED from the hospital, my father kicked me out. I went to my aunt's house with Sia and begged her to let me stay with her. Soon afterward, she called my stepmother and began to argue with her over what had happened. My father and stepmother threatened my aunt, and she took me back home.

It was unbearable living in that house, looking at that boy, and knowing that my parents didn't believe me. My days descended back into the hell of living in the basement. My stepmother called from work one day, asking me to do some chores around the house, but I was taking care of the baby and I didn't get to finish. When she arrived home, she was so upset that she and my father kicked me out again.

I had nowhere to go and no idea what to do. I called my ESL teacher from Richfield Junior High. So I called her. She came and picked up Sia and I and took us to her home. She introduced us to her husband and grown children, and we all cooked dinner and played games. It was there that Sia was given the nickname Sarah. My ESL teacher told me that we could stay until she could get hold of the shelter for teenage mothers.

Once they returned her call, she drove the baby and I to downtown Minneapolis. When we got there, they showed me my room and laid out the rules of the shelter. My baby and I settled in for the night.

The next morning, I was given my chores to do around the shelter and told about the services they would provide. For the first week, I cried every day. This was not the future I wanted. The neighborhood was pretty rough. I tried to get into the routine and fit in, but no matter what I did, I couldn't fit in with these girls. They could read and write and speak English better than I could. They had nice clothes, and they were pretty. I couldn't read or write, and I didn't have nice clothes or a job. I was in a strange land, a permanent visitor with no family. I was lost with a child.

TWELVE

THREE WEEKS INTO MY TIME at the shelter, I took Sia to the corner store to buy some candy. On my way back to the shelter, a black vehicle pulled up beside the curb. A man leaned out and called, "What's up, shorty?"

"I'm not your shorty," I retorted. I kept walking, but he followed me. I stopped and talked to him.

"Where do you live?" he asked.

"At the shelter."

"What's a beautiful girl like you doing at the shelter with a baby?"

I told him that my parents had kicked me out. He gave me his number and told me to call him.

A few days later, I called. He told me he was going to pick me and the baby up so we could spend some time together. I told him that would be fine, and he picked us up that afternoon. He introduced himself as we climbed into the car; his real name was Chris, he said, but he had a street name.

After going out to eat, he took the baby and I to his family's house. At first I didn't understand because this house was packed with both children and adults. That very night, he told me to go get my stuff from the shelter and move in with him. This didn't seem like the ideal living situation, but Chris was very nice to the baby and me, and I desperately needed someone to help me take care of her, so I accepted.

Chris seemed to float in and out of the house day and night, and so did everyone else. I found out soon that both he and his cousin were selling drugs. One day he introduced me to his Aunt Nancy, who had come over to visit her sister. She asked me where I was from, and I told her West Africa. She told me she liked my accent. At that time my English was horrible, so I found this funny.

Nancy became a true friend. She was kind and caring, and she always looked out for Sia and me. She and I clicked right from the start, and I began going over to her house frequently. It was a very small house, not far from the shelter.

One morning, Nancy came to pick me up from Chris' house. We drove around for about three hours, looking at garage sales. When we got back to her house, she got a call saying Chris had been shot in a drive-by shooting. Panicked, we ran over to the house. They told us that Chris had been pronounced dead.

Oh my God! This can't be happening. My first real boyfriend, the father figure to my child—dead. *Why does bad luck follow me? Why am I cursed?* Had I been cursed by the people I stole from to help my mother's addiction? Had I offended some evil spirit? I felt the loss for Chris' family, and I missed him so badly it tore me apart. Through my tears of sorrow, I also realized I was back to being homeless.

After Chris' funeral, to my surprise, Nancy asked me to move in with her. Her three girls were not happy with their mother. Nancy took me in and drove me around to churches to get food, diapers, and clothes. Sometimes we took all day going places to get free food, clothes, household supplies, anything you can think of. Nancy also took me to the government center in downtown Minneapolis to apply for cash assistance and food stamps. I was finally able to buy food for Sia and I. I could finally buy her nice clothes and tiny shoes for her little feet.

Nancy put me in a school that had a program for teenage mothers. Sia and I got on the school bus together in the morning. Imagine trying to get yourself and your baby dressed so you can catch the school bus at seven in the morning. I felt so stupid getting on that bus; it was embarrassing being the only teenager with a baby. But I did it.

When I get to school, I would drop Sia off at daycare and then go to class. One of the classes was designed to teach us how to be parents. After school, I picked Sia up from daycare and got back on the school bus. I wanted so much to not be tied down to a baby, but at this point I had no choice.

I'm not sure if my parents ever looked for me, but one day I called them and let them know I was living with Nancy and going to school. Soon afterward, they came to visit and didn't think it was a good neighborhood or decent living situation. They called Nancy to tell her they wanted me to move back home. I begged Nancy not to take me back to my parents. Nancy said regretfully that she had no guardianship over me, and since I was underage, she had to do as my parents asked. I regretted making that phone call with all my being.

THIRTEEN

WHEN SIA WAS FOUR MONTHS OLD, I moved back to my parents' house. When I got there, it seems my father had a plan. He told me that I was to take my baby to Africa so that my mother's sister, Auntie Buwa Gibson, could raise the child. I was to come back and go to school. I agreed.

My father worked for Northwest Airlines at the time, so he worked quickly to get a passport for the baby and standby tickets. When Sia was almost five months old, we landed in Ghana, where we were picked up by Auntie Buwa Gibson.

The next day, I explained everything to her. She told me she would raise the baby. As required, we went to the American embassy to let them know there was an American citizen in the country, just in case something were to happen.

Per my father's instructions, I called him from the embassy as well. My father asked me to give the phone to the staff member. The next thing I knew, this man had taken my passport and everything else on me. I protested, but he told me to leave.

In a panic, I called my father again. "Father, the man at the embassy took my passport!"

"I know, Charlesetta."

I was stunned. "But I won't be able to get back into the United States—"

"You're not coming back to the United States."

The line went dead. I drew the receiver away from my ear and stared at it, shocked and confused.

That was the last time I spoke to my father.

FOURTEEN

ONCE WE RETURNED HOME, Auntie Buwa said, "Leave the baby and go see your grandmother and your mother in Liberia."

I was excited; I hadn't seen my grandmother since the last war. I boarded a bus to travel to Liberia. As I crossed the border, however, I began to feel as though I were watching a movie. Bad memories of my mother kept flashing through my mind; bad memories of the war and the things I had gone through as a child soldier ricocheted behind my closed eyes.

When I got to the family compound everyone was excited to see me. When I saw my grandmother, we both broke down crying. She hugged me tight, kissing my cheek, and I could feel the warmth of her thin body as she held on to me.

"Are you hungry?" she asked, her eyes bright with happiness.

"Yes. Is everyone else home?"

As usual, my siblings were in the backyard playing while my mother was out getting drunk. My grandmother eased my disappointment, however, by ushering me inside, where she began to make my favorite food. I ate with my siblings and my grandmother as we talked loudly, laughing at the good memories and talking solemnly about the bad. Looking at my grandmother, I could still see the loving glow in her eyes. Things were so different; the war had changed so much for my family, but some things would never change. For the first time in a long time, despite the circumstances, I felt I was home.

• • •

Here she comes, the black sheep of the family. In the middle of the night she crashed in, screaming "I hear my daughter is back! Darlene! Where are you?" I woke from my sleep with a start, staring into the pitch black and dreading seeing her again.

I heard my grandmother say in a low voice, "She's sleeping, baby girl. Go to sleep now. When you wake up in the morning, you will see your daughter."

There was the sound of stumbling feet. "No. I want to see her now."

In my grandmother's bed, I screwed my eyes tightly closed and pretended to be asleep. I heard her stumble against the doorway and stare in at me, breathing heavily; then, to my surprise, she turned away and went to her bed.

The next morning was as bad as I feared. The moment she woke up, her face twisted into a smile. "Come here."

I obeyed.

"I heard your father deported you and you have a baby."

"Quit questioning her, Onike," my grandmother broke in. "She just got here after a long car ride."

Believe it or not, I was still afraid of my mother. It had been two and a half years since I had seen her; I had grown into an adult, but some old fears never die. I had wondered, on the long trip, if I should give her a hug, but my hopes were dashed as soon as I saw her. I could see that she hadn't changed.

It didn't matter who treated me like a princess in my family's home; it didn't matter that the people in my old hometown treated me so nicely, knowing I had come from America. Everyone wanted to talk to the "American girl"—I could do no wrong. Everything I asked for was given to me, with the exception of my mother's love. She was still the same old drunk; the only thing that had improved, or so I heard, was her level of skill in the criminal arts. She now had a master's degree in conning people.

Soon after I arrived, she had the audacity to ask me if I had brought any money. When I told her I hadn't, she went to the room I shared with her and my siblings and began unpacking the clothes I had brought from America. She emptied them onto the floor, rummaged through the pile, and took all the best ones. I stood by silently, angry with myself for being afraid.

FIFTEEN

AFTER A FEW MONTHS IN LIBERIA, my family and friends started asking me when I was coming back to the United States. As far as they knew, I had brought my baby back and was planning to return soon. I was too ashamed to tell anyone I wasn't going back to the United States; I simply changed the subject when anyone asked, or shrugged and said I hadn't booked my flight back yet.

After six months I went from being the American girl that everybody wanted to be around to the subject of rumors and gossip. People in town, even family and friends, said that I had been deported for prostitution, drug trafficking, or being a gangster. Others hissed that they had heard I had been sleeping with married men; my father had deported me so I wasn't killed by their wives. I knew who was to blame for the rumors. Once again, my mother was controlling my life.

My mother wasn't physically abusive toward me anymore—maybe she had decided I was too big now to bully—but she was verbally abusive.

I started going to church with my mother every Wednesday and Sunday. This church was more based on reading into your future than any I had attended in the past. They spoke in tongues, and the parishioners claimed to see things that the normal eyes couldn't see. There was a lot of singing and dancing. One Wednesday, my sister, my mother, and I went to church. After dancing and singing, we were told to pray out loud and talk to God about our heart's desire. Standing beside my mother, I was overcome with emotion. I cried and prayed out loud to God, asking for help.

Suddenly, the young pastor of the church called out, "Stop praying! I have received a message from God." As I watched, stunned, he came forward and stood beside my mother. "Sister Onike, the Lord says you are going to be my wife."

As I stared in shock, the voices of the congregation rose in delight. Everybody started praying and rejoicing in "the revelation." My mother sobbed, a smile spreading wide across her face, as she thanked God.

That's how my mother and Mr. Thomas came to be married. She immediately moved him in to the bedroom she shared with her four children.

At first I was happy about the marriage. My mother looked happy for the first time in a long time. Maybe, I thought, being a pastor's wife would change her ways. I had started dating one of my grandmother's renters, so I started spending the night with him to leave the room for my mother and Mr. Thomas. I was kind to him each day, and he seemed like an upstanding man.

As time went by, however, I began to realize incredulously that he was nothing but a criminal. As I watched, he and my mother used the church to further their schemes, taking advantage of believers. They charged people for holy oil, claiming that they could influence God to help the parishioners, but only if they were willing to make a sacrifice and donate to the church. They lined their own pockets with the money. At night, my mother stumbled home drunk—with Mr. Thomas right behind her.

The nightmare soon spread beyond the church. When Mr. Thomas learned of the extent of my mother's scams, he became fully involved. Together they scammed thousands of dollars from potential renters. They lied, straight-faced, knowing that they had no property to rent. After a scamming spree, they skipped town with the three kids.

I took over my mother's room, miserable. My mother and I had a bad reputation around town; I was lonely and missed my brothers and sisters. I wondered about my baby every day. I had a hot meal every day, thanks to my beloved grandmother, but I began to sink slowly and seemingly irretrievably toward depression.

SIXTEEN

ONE DAY MY LUCK CHANGED. I was sitting on the porch, staring out into the road, when I spotted a handsome man—Nigerian, I could tell—making his way toward me. Well-dressed and walking confidently, he made his way up the front porch steps. His voice was smooth as velvet.

"Excuse me, do you know where Sister Comfort is?"

Sister Comfort was one of my grandmother's tenants. My grandmother emerged, inviting the man in and asking me to go get Sister Comfort.

Once we came back, Sister Comfort properly introduced the gentleman to me. To my surprise, I realized that he had actually come to see me. She had asked him to come, thinking he might like me, but had forgotten to tell me about the setup.

I was overcome with anxiety. He was in a suit and tie; I looked like a mess. I didn't look like anything this man should be dating. Each time he came to see me, we met in Sister Comfort's room to talk.

One day, he asked to go to my room. I told old him I had nothing in it, not even a bed. I explained my situation to him.

When he was about to leave, he pressed something into my palm. My eyes widened as I looked down: it was five hundred American dollars.

"To fix up your room," he said, smiling.

In my country that's a lot of money. I thanked him profusely, and that very afternoon, went shopping like a big girl. I bought furniture, food, nice clothes, and new shoes. I was able to give my grandmother five thousand Liberian dollars.

I felt on top of the word. Finally, I had a sense of security. I was surrounded by beautiful things. I felt fine, and loved, and mature. My eyes felt as though they had finally opened.

When he came back to visit, I took him proudly to my new room. I pulled him down to sit and thanked him again for the money. "I don't know where you got it, but thank you, thank you for giving it to me."

A smile played over his handsome face. "Do you know who I am?"

"Yes!" I exclaimed. "Well . . . I know . . . that you are from Nigeria. I guess that's all I know."

He laughed. "Yes, I am. But I bet you didn't know that I'm the president's bodyguard."

Now I understood the fancy suits and tie. I understood the money, and why he always carried a gun. I was proud of my new man, and word slowly spread around town. I never knew when he was coming to visit; he popped up to see me unexpectedly after work, and I felt the jealousy of the other girls in town when I described the importance of what he did in Nigeria.

I was living it up. I was finally grown up, and I had everyone respecting me again. I had food, nice clothes, and money to spend. I wasn't worried about all the problems I had left back in the United States, or my baby in Ghana. My troubles were a world away.

SEVENTEEN

IT WAS INEVITABLE THAT, being young and dumb, I would let my success go to my head. I was dating a man who was doing everything for me, who loved me, and I was happier than I had ever been.

And yet dissatisfaction began to creep in. Boredom reared its head, and I began to notice my ex-boyfriend coming and going from the house he rented from my grandmother. One day I followed him home, driven by lust, and we slept together. Despite the tinge of guilt I felt, I wanted more. I loved the forbidden feeling of the affair. We began sleeping together regularly.

One day, my grandmother was out shopping and the little kids were in the house. Behind the locked door of my bedroom, my ex-boyfriend and I were having sex. Suddenly, I overheard a familiar voice talking to one of the children at the door. It was my boyfriend.

"Oh my God," I whispered to my ex-boyfriend. "Go out the window."

He pointed to the steel bars over the window. I leaned over and peered under the bed, but I knew he would never fit. "Okay. I'm going to hide in my closet. You open the door and tell him I'm not here. Tell him you were just fixing something in my room, and then lock the door when he leaves."

I leapt into the closet and hid myself behind the hanging clothes as he dressed. Listening closely, I heard my ex-boyfriend explain that he was my grandmother's tenant and was fixing the door, but I wasn't home.

"That's alright. You can just leave the bedroom door open. I'll sit and wait for her." His voice sounded hard.

He knows I'm here.

"Listen," my ex-boyfriend said, "I don't know you, and I don't want to get in trouble for leaving the door open. You can come back later." I heard the door close and the lock click into place.

Thank God. Just as I was thinking the words, I heard a loud crash that could only be the door flying off its hinges. *Oh my God. He kicked the door in.* My ex-boyfriend began to swear loudly.

"Come out," my boyfriend called loudly. "I know you're here, Charles-etta." I hunched lower in the closet, hand pressed over my mouth. I heard another sound, the click of a gun safety going off. "If you don't come out, I'm going to start shooting everywhere in this room."

I erupted forth from the closet, screaming for him to stop.

He stared at me, a deranged look of anger warping his face. "Give me one reason why I shouldn't shoot you."

I started crying and pleading for his forgiveness. Mid-plea, my grand-mother walked in.

"Hey," he said calmly in greeting.

Her eyes flicked from his face to the gun to me to my ex-boyfriend, unable to process the situation.

She pleaded with him, and he finally left.

That very night he came back with some friends, looking for my ex-boyfriend, who had wisely skipped town for the night. I knew that was the end of the president's bodyguard and me. I also knew that I had undeniably, and irrevocably, fucked up.

EIGHTEEN

A MONTH LATER, I crept into the house around dawn with nothing but five dollars in my pocket. I felt drunk and tired. I submerged myself in the bathtub, brooding, and then left to spend the five dollars on food.

As I sat on the porch eating, frustrated and resigning myself to a day spent home in bed, my grandmother came to the doorway and saw me. A look of disgust crept over her face.

"You go out all night and let men use you, and all you have to show to for it is a coldbowl?" She stared out at me and my fast food for a long moment. Then she turned to go back inside, spitting over her shoulder, "Coldbowls are for prostitutes."

I watched her receding back, eyebrows raised, spoon hanging midway over my breakfast. *What's wrong with her? She never talks like that.*

And for sure, something was wrong with my grandmother. Later that afternoon, she had visitors from the church. I heard them praying in my grandmother's room, and then they passed me silently as she walked them back to the road. When she came back, I was still sitting on the porch, staring out over the palms. As she passed me, I snapped from my daze to see her falling to the floor. Launching myself from my chair, I caught her instinctively, and she landed on my lap. I stared down in horror. Foam was dripping from her mouth, and her eyes were rolling in her head. Her legs shook violently as her hand clenched involuntarily, seeming to crawl in on itself. Something told me to straighten her hand as I began screaming for help. The church members raced back up the road and helped get her to the hospital.

It didn't matter what I had been through before. My mind raced in panic. I couldn't lose her, the one person who loved me, the one person who cared for me. It was one of the scariest days of my life. When my grandma arrived at the hospital, Auntie Buwa, who was the head of the family, came down and took my grandmother up to Ghana.

I strongly believe that God used me that day to save my grandmother's life. Any other day I would have been gone. I was never a homebody; I didn't wallow, miserable as I was, but went out. But for some reason, God kept me at home that day.

All the same, that was the last time I ever saw my grandmother alive. She died soon afterward, and her body was sent back to Liberia so that she could be buried next to her husband and her daughter. The church and street were packed with people paying their respects, and all the grandchildren walked beside her body while we brought her to her final resting place. It was a long walk, made longer by my dread of the days to come. Because I knew that when she had died, the family compound, my whole way of life, had died with her.

NINETEEN

WE WERE ALL ON OUR OWN once she died. There was no more grandmother to keep the family together; there were no more hot meals, no more sympathetic ears. There was no one to care for the family compound, to clean the home or worry when I stayed out at night. I had no one to turn to.

I couldn't read or write, so job prospects were low. I had to put food in my mouth somehow, and the only way I could think to do it was to begin keeping two lovers at the same time. It wasn't prostitution, I thought uneasily, although I cared for neither. Both were known around town as losers, but no one had to know; I had to eat.

Desperate for another way, I went looking for my mother. I uneasily approached the door, knocked, and asked for some rice and money. She shook her head.

"You need to do what the other girls are doing to help their mothers."

"What's that?"

"Selling sex for money," she responded.

"No," I said firmly. "No." My grandmother would have been ashamed to hear the words. My mother had ruined everything for me; I was furious. She couldn't make me do this.

With a straight face, she responded, "Look at these girls your own age. They have a nice place. They helped *their* mother." I stared at her, incredulous. She continued calmly, "They sleep with government officials, businessmen, or rich white men. You could do the same. You're here begging me for food, when you're the one supposed to be bringing it to me."

I turned on my heel, without a response, and returned home angrily. But there wasn't any food there. I was alone with my thoughts, my growling stomach, and the panic of not knowing how to survive.

Maybe Onike was right.

• • •

I found my first customer on the street. He drove a beautiful car. He pulled over, we made a deal, and we had sex in the car. Afterward, he told me to wait there and that he would return with my money. He left me stranded.

My next client was the judge. Every time I went to see him, we had sex in his office, his friend's house, or in a building that had been burned down in the war. He paid me well enough that I could put food on the table without sleeping with anyone else.

One day, talking with friends in town, I overheard someone gossiping about the judge's former lovers. Amused, I began to listen in. And then I heard one name that made my blood run cold.

Next time we entered the burned-out building, I pushed him back. "Wait. I need to ask you something. Did you used to sleep with Onike?"

"Yes, I used to have sex with your mother." He watched as a look of horror came over my face, then broke into a wicked smile. "But it's not a problem. I like you better."

Disgust flooded through me. I stared at him, trying to swallow my pride, but I realized suddenly that I couldn't do it. Prostitution wasn't for me. I turned my back on the judge and his money and fled through the charred doorway. I didn't stop running until I got home.

TWENTY

AFTER MY QUICK FORAY into the world of prostitution, I got involved in a whole lot of dead-end relationships.

The turmoil finally halted on my nineteenth birthday, February 10, 2000, when I met Anthony. He owned a liquor store in the center of town, and my friends and I went to his shop to celebrate. During the celebration, I could see him glancing over at me from behind the counter. I had never seen him before; I ignored the glances and laughed with my friends. He wasn't my type.

When I left, though, Anthony told me to come back the following night to see him. I decided to make the effort; I couldn't see any way out of my situation without a man, and here was one who owned his own business. I came back the next night, and Anthony and I spent the night on the floor of the shop.

As I left the next morning, Anthony pulled a wad of cash out of his drawer and peeled out one hundred US dollars. I left the shop ecstatic, stuffing the money down into my pockets. He may not have been my type—I had no feelings for him whatsoever—but he could offer me stability and safety, and that was most important. I began going to Anthony's shop every day. I would leave with a few new bills each time, enough to buy food and take care of my day-to-day needs.

Before I knew it, I was pregnant. We decided I would have an abortion.

We soon fell into a comfortable routine. I managed to overlook my initial feelings against Anthony. Originally from Nigeria, he had moved here to work, and that was all he did. He worked all day and then slept in his shop; he had no type of social life. He wore the same dirty, worn clothes all the time, only changing into clean clothes on Sundays. I was embarrassed to bring him around my friends. But as time passed, we grew more serious. I needed money, and Anthony provided for me very well; he had money to spare from the shop. But all that was threatened at the idea of me being pregnant.

Soon, it seemed like I was pregnant every time I turned around. Over the next few months, I had two more abortions.

A few months later, I walked to the shop with panic rising inside me and a ringing in my head. I knew it was happening again; I was pregnant. I couldn't believe it had happened for the fourth time. I told Anthony with dread, but his face softened. "Why don't we keep it?" he asked. "Maybe it's meant to be."

Maybe it was. So I carried the pregnancy through full term and, a few months later, I had a baby girl.

TWENTY-ONE

IT WARMED MY HEART to see Anthony with the baby. She was his first child, and he doted on her, carrying her around and smiling into her tiny face. He was a good father and a good provider. He had soon built a bedroom onto the back of his shop so the baby and I could live with him.

At this point in my life I had given up all hope of going back to America. My father hadn't contacted me since dropping me off at the airport. I had no money aside from Anthony, who wanted me here, and no foreseeable way to escape. The only family I saw frequently was my mother, who dropped in unannounced with the sole purpose, it seemed, of insulting me. So I decided to make the best of my situation and play house with Anthony. I started helping out with his business, and in an effort to support him and make more money, I opened my own business beside the shop.

Though I felt it a good step toward financial security, it soon became apparent that my family and friends thought my owning the business was embarrassing and degrading. My mother was at the forefront of this vicious tide of gossip. Whenever she'd visit, she'd hiss, "Look at you. You were an *American* girl. You come here from America and have a baby with this dirty Nigerian boy when you could have been dating executives. You ruined your chances."

I tried to keep Anthony out of earshot when my mother stopped by, but one day I came home to find her berating him. "You have to pay a bride price for my daughter. If you want to keep her here in this shop, you're going to marry her."

"I don't want to get married," I protested as I came through the doorway, stepping between her and Anthony.

"Charlesetta, I'm trying to make this man see that you are from a respectable family. He doesn't respect you, no one in the family respects you, and I don't respect you. If you marry him, everyone will respect you."

I shook my head. I knew that was a scam. When she left, Anthony tried to discuss the marriage with me, but I cut him off. It wasn't going to happen.

• • •

When you have a mother like mine, resolutions don't last long. She showed up each day, clearly smelling a way to get some more money, obsessively driven. She followed me in the street, barking about respect. She came over to hold the baby and whispered to Anthony that I might return to America someday, and if we were married, he would be able to join me. She hung around the shop harassing me day in and day out.

When she took upon herself to schedule a traditional marriage ceremony, I went along with it miserably. Anthony agreed eagerly. He loved me and the baby, and my mother's whispers about a new life in America, no matter how unlikely I protested they were, always put a gleam into his eyes.

The day of the marriage was upon me sooner than I would have liked. We had family and friends gather, and I prepared a lot of food and poured drinks for everyone. My mother and her husband received six thousand dollars plus some gifts from Anthony and his family. I watched her out of the corner of my eye, laughing and talking with the guests, and bitter hatred rose up within me.

As I had predicted, the wedding was the last time I saw my mother. She and her husband took the money and moved to Ghana with it. She didn't come over to say goodbye or leave any forwarding address.

I was married to a man I didn't love, running a business I didn't want, and was confined to the house with a newborn baby. But at least I had food to eat, and at least that woman was finally out of my life.

TWENTY-TWO

YOU CAN GET USED TO a loveless marriage like you can get used to anything else. Anthony, the baby, and I went on with our daily life, and I was surprised at how easy everything had become. His business was doing well, and my little side business was even bringing in some money. Life had become like a comfortable dream.

The dream shattered in 2003 with the start of the April 6 War. We had heard rumblings throughout the town about rebels approaching; the previous week a deadly quiet had fallen over the neighborhood. We were on alert, eyes open, uneasy. As I came through the front door of the shop, I saw a stream of people moving down the street, running, yelling, carrying luggage on their heads.

Oh my God. This can't actually be happening.

One neighbor stopped in the shop, weighed down with clothing and blankets. "Why are you still here? The rebels are approaching this area," he said in a panic, then darted back out toward the street.

Anthony hesitated. If we left, we could lose everything in his shop.

I went into the back bedroom, grabbed the baby and began to dress her, calling out firmly that we needed to leave right now. Anthony packed a few personal items and anything valuable that he could grab, carrying a small mattress in one hand and balancing our luggage on his head with the other as I tied the baby to my back. We locked up the business hurriedly, then began to run, plunging out into the crowd of people moving toward the other side of town.

It took us all day to walk to our destination, an area of town where we had heard there would be peacekeepers. But as soon as we were no longer physically in danger, we began to worry. What if the rebels were able to make it to this side of town?

After a few weeks, a cease-fire was called. The peacekeepers announced that it was safe for us to return to our homes. We set off toward the other side of town in dread, having no idea what we would find when we got there.

• • •

The shop was an empty shell. The rebels had stolen everything but the walls themselves. Trash and glass lay scattered over the floor, the shelves pulled down, bullet holes marking the walls of the surrounding buildings. I turned to Anthony but couldn't say a word. He looked crushed; his face was ashen. He sat down on the floor and put his head in his hands. After a few minutes, he said in a low voice, "We don't have a penny to our names."

Over the next few days, as I unpacked and tried to clean up the ruined shop, Anthony started to think of some ideas. He began bagging water to sell to neighbors. I helped him, preparing the bags and hauling water up while the baby was asleep, but we weren't getting anywhere. Our neighbors were consumed with getting their own lives back together; no one had any money to spare.

After several days, we visited my cousin in hopes that he could spare us some money. He couldn't. On our way back home, however, we saw some people pulling tubs filled with ice up the hill. Anthony went to talk with one of them, and they directed us toward a building at the bottom of the hill, where there was a large building wired with electricity. Anthony made a deal with the owner and brought our refrigerator down to the building to make use of the electricity.

So started our ice business. We rose early in the morning and spent all day bagging water and hauling the heavy bags out to the freezer. After two days, the water would have frozen. We then packed the ice into tubs and pulled it up to the large red-light market in town. Sometimes, when business was good, we would make two to three trips with tubs full of ice to sell. But business was usually hard to find; there were usually about ten other people trying to sell ice at the same time. Anthony and I raised our voices louder over everyone else, trying to get the customers' attention first, calling out that we could offer a deal. When that didn't work, I pulled the bin around the market, desperately trying to make contact with customers before the ice melted in the heat.

Though we had started to scratch out a living, Anthony remained tight with his money. Gone were the days of hundred-dollar bills. He told me that I didn't need to wash my clothes as often; I was wearing them out. I felt dirty and resentful. I began begging family members for their unwanted clothing.

Life had turned around on me again, and I didn't like what I saw.

TWENTY-THREE

AFTER A FEW MONTHS of hauling ice back and forth, Anthony's stinginess finally paid off. He saved up a little money and opened a new shop in Conga Town. Once again, we were sleeping in the back of a shop with nothing in it.

My clothes were torn and dirty; I avoided family and friends in embarrassment. Miserable, I started to sleep with other men for what they could give me. I scraped a little money together and started my own business selling roasted fish and meat in the market at night.

One day in the market, I ran into my aunt, who told me that my paternal grandfather had returned from America. He wasn't doing well, she said; he was very sick and had only returned because he didn't want to die in America. My eagerness to see him turned into shock and sadness at the news.

A few days later, I went to visit him at my aunt's house. He looked small and frail in the large bed. He smiled as I gave him a hug.

"I came back to see you and our family," he started. "I've been begging your father to bring you back to the United States. I've missed you."

We talked for some time about my father and the rest of the family, and I told him about all that had happened since I had come home. As I told the story, I was overcome was disappointment and relief at seeing him again. Tears welled up in my eyes.

$$\bullet \ \bullet \ \bullet$$

Two months later, my grandfather passed away.

We kept the body for thirty days, which is a tradition for us. People came in and out of the home to grieve with us at all hours. The house filled with the warm smells of cooking and the sounds of sobbing in the living room. The men gathered in the corner, talking in low voices about the funeral arrangements.

At grandfather's funeral, I represented my father, as he couldn't be there and I was his oldest daughter. After we buried him, I moved back to the family compound on Lane Street.

Three months later, I got a message that my father wanted to talk to me. Filled with anxiety and hope at the same time, I went down to the telecommunication office in town to talk with him. His voice sounded different than I remembered, and I was filled with emotion as soon as I heard it. He told me he was going to send some money, for me to go to Ghana and get my passport. I was then to return to the United States.

A week later, I received the money and secretly bought my bus ticket to Ghana. I told no one except for my cousin, and I made her swear not to say anything to anyone about where I had gone. Early that morning, I crept out of the house, my baby on my back, and boarded the bus. It was hot and overcrowded; we were squished together on the hard seats. But as I watched the dust of the old town recede through the window, I had never felt so free.

TWENTY-FOUR

WHEN MY DAUGHTER AND I arrived safely in Ghana, I was reunited with Sia. I stayed in Ghana with my aunt for a month, waiting on my documentation to come so that I could leave for the United States.

My aunt pressured me from the beginning to go spend time with my mother before leaving the country. I refused repeatedly; I knew nothing good would come of it. But she kept insisting. I finally caved. Maybe there was a way to get some closure, to get through to my mother, and to see my siblings one last time before I left Africa for good.

Once again, I found my mother in a one-bedroom home with her husband and three children. I decided to stay for a few days for the sake of my siblings. It was amazing to laugh with them, to spend time with them, to act as though nothing terrible had happened within my broken family.

Not surprisingly, things soon went downhill. One morning a few days into my stay, I walked into the bedroom without knocking and stumbled upon Mr. Thomas changing. I ducked my head and quickly ran back out, mumbling that I was sorry.

Apparently an apology wasn't enough. Mr. Thomas told my mother right away. She began swearing and cursing right away. Leaning in close to my face, she spat, "You might want a husband, but my husband doesn't want you."

The next day I went to the market to purchase some African clothes, slippers, and souvenirs to bring to my stepmother and my father. If I was going to start over in America, I wanted to start off on a good note.

When I arrived home and set down my bags, my mother picked them all up and took them back into the bedroom. As I stared after her, she popped her head out and snarled, "I'm keeping all this. You can go back to your Auntie Buwa's house now. I don't want you here anymore."

I sat, fists closed tightly, and debated whether to fight her, to go after the bags of clothing. Finally, I rose silently, hugged my siblings, turned, and walked out the door. I knew it was the last time I would see her or Mr. Thomas.

TWENTY-FIVE

WHEN I ARRIVED AT the Minneapolis International Airport, I found my father, stepmother Sia, and younger brother Ceephas waiting for me there. The reunion with my parents was awkward. As soon as I saw them, the anger I had felt toward them came rushing back, but at the same time, I was grateful for the chance to begin a new future in the United States. I also missed my baby, whom I had left with Auntie Buwa Gibson to ease my transition into the United States.

It was 2003, several years since I had left, and I was excited to be back. The air felt much colder than in Africa, but fresh and exciting. As I climbed into the car, I stared out the window at the world around me, relishing the sight of the green trees and neat rows of homes flying by. As we pulled up to the home, I grew more nervous. It was the same home I had been raped in, tried to hang myself in. I shivered as the memories came back.

I was introduced in the doorway to my two other siblings by marriage. They were my stepmother's children, who had come from Africa.

Then I saw him. My throat filled with a sour taste and my heart pounded. The father of my child, the cause of my misery, my half brother. He looked me in the eye and said hello, and I felt the white heat of anger rising up within me. He still lived in the home; I was going to have to stay under the same roof with him. I was going to have to play happy family in the same home, knowing all the while what he had done.

It turned out that school wasn't much better. I didn't know how to read, and I didn't know any of the other students. Teachers didn't seem to know what to do with me. I sat alone at lunch, staring straight ahead and feeling loneliness in the pit of my stomach. I snapped at teachers and yelled at other students, frustrated and afraid.

At home, the whole family still seemed to be judging me. My siblings were close, but I couldn't seem to get into their inner circle. I felt like an outcast. No matter what I did, they seemed to think I had put a curse on the family.

I was being crushed under the weight of my own low self-esteem. I didn't trust any of them; I had to avoid my half brother at all costs while maintaining a façade of normalcy around the others. I knew I hadn't done anything wrong, but the constant distrustful looks and awkward silences made me question everything I said and did.

Desperate, one afternoon I brought home a boy I had met at school, introducing him as my baby's father. If they thought I had cursed the family, I would remove the curse myself. Maybe they would go along with my lie. My siblings would look at me with love and trust, and my parents would stop hating me.

That didn't work so well, because I knew the truth, and so did my parents. I couldn't pretend to lie, and they couldn't pretend to think of me as anything more than the black sheep of a daughter who had wreaked havoc on their happy home.

I couldn't pretend that I didn't think about killing my half brother each time I looked at him. No matter how I tried to avoid him, the house just wasn't big enough. Every time I saw him my brain spun off into darkness, thinking about shooting him, the satisfaction of stabbing him, how I'd like to hear him scream in pain. When my parents spoke to me, I snapped back at them. Fed up with my siblings, I picked fights. My hopes were crumbling; I couldn't see myself getting along with any of them.

When they finally kicked me out of the house, I was glad.

TWENTY-SIX

RELIEVED AS I WAS that I wouldn't have to live in that household anymore, I didn't know where I was going to go. I dreaded the idea of returning to the filthy shelter. I slammed the front door behind me and began pacing down the sidewalk, my mind racing over what to do next. Angry tears streamed down my face between my fingers.

"You okay?"

My eyes met those of an older man walking a large dog.

"No. My family hates me and they're kicking me out of the house. I don't have anywhere to go." Before I knew it, the tears were coming harder. I talked fast, telling him the whole story, begging him for an answer.

When I had finished, he looked at me a long moment and introduced himself as Joe. He told me I could stay with him, and that I should pack up and come to his cousin Terry's house with him. In no place to refuse such an offer, I accepted. It wasn't far to Terry's place, where he lived with his girlfriend. Just across the way from Terry's was Joe's place. Joe had lived alone until I moved in.

I earned my keep at Joe's by helping him around the house with the cooking and cleaning. Joe worked all day, but when he returned, his home would turn into a hangout spot for friends. It was a fun place to stay. There were always people coming and going, never a dull moment. I began to grow closer with Joe as time passed. These two men rescued me from a terrible situation when I was just twenty years old.

I soon heard that Terry acted as a pimp for a few women. He introduced them to paying clients to have sex with and take a little off the top of the rate they charged. He turned a decent profit. One day, overcome by curiosity about how it worked, I went with two girls to a client's house. I sat there uncomfortably, watching both girls have sex with the men right next to each other. I was struck by how easygoing and bold the girls were. I was too shy ever to get involved in that lifestyle; I couldn't imagine it.

But I liked the girls. It was refreshing to be around people who weren't judgmental or rude. They accepted me as I was and genuinely liked me. I began to hang out with them everywhere they went, even going to clients' homes more regularly.

I had been attending school all through this time, but overcome by bitterness and frustration, I walked out the door one day and didn't go back. I felt useless sitting in a classroom, being berated by teachers and classmates all day. I didn't need an education. I would find another way to make money.

The girls introduced me to their friend who, I found out later on, dressed in drag at night. He introduced us to boosting, or shoplifting, from the mall and then reselling the products on the street. I started boosting almost every day to get by, selling everything from clothing to DVDs to electronics on the street.

I had begun sleeping with Joe, and I could tell he had begun to fall hard for me. But deep within me, I felt a gnawing ache. I wanted Terry. I was grateful to Joe for taking me into his home, and I cared about him. Terry had a girlfriend, pimped out women for cash, and had a steady stream of unsavory visitors in and out of his home. But I couldn't help it; I was so strongly attracted to him that I was starting to feel uncomfortable. I had no direction; I didn't know where I was going with my life. All I knew was that I needed a way out, but couldn't think of one. I start doing things that I shouldn't do.

TWENTY-SEVEN

ONE MORNING I GOT A CALL from my friend Woode. We had been close in my hometown in Africa. It was amazing to hear her voice again. She had moved to the United States, she said, a few weeks ago, but had been kicked out of her home. She didn't know anyone and didn't have anywhere to go.

I asked Joe if Woode could move in. He seemed hesitant to take in someone else without a job, but when I begged him, his eyes softened and he agreed. If my friend needed help, he said, she was his friend too.

The next two weeks were pure happiness. Woode and I sat and talked at the kitchen table while Joe was at work. We took walks and explored the neighborhood. I introduced her to Terry and they hit it off. At night, I whispered my fears to her, the guilt I felt about Joe, the problems with Terry, everything that had been weighing me down about school and my family. She spilled her own heavy story: thrown into a new city where she didn't know the language, impatient relatives, angry teachers. I felt light as air. I wasn't the only one who was living this way.

TWENTY-EIGHT

WHEN JOE CAME IN the front door crying, I knew the decision had been made for me. He had lost his job; ringing his hands, he angrily recounted the layoffs in his office. He wouldn't have the money for rent, and Terry didn't have enough to cover him. He was going to lose the apartment, he said, staring at the floor.

Woode packed her things and headed for Missouri, where she had some other relatives. I felt empty as I hugged her goodbye and watched her figure receding down the street, suitcase in tow, looking small. I didn't know where to go.

At church, I asked my pastor for advice. Later the same week, he set me up with a church member who had agreed to take me in. It was a relief to know that there were good, kind people out there who would take a risk on me.

Gary was an older man, thin and balding, who was like a father figure to me. He spoke in a low, soft voice and had kind eyes. He took on a teacher role as soon as I moved in, explaining how things worked in town, where to look for a job, and how to make myself presentable in interviews. Before I knew it, I had landed a job.

As an engineer, Gary worked long hours. I was often home alone, and on some days, I would invite boys I had met at work or other friends from my old neighborhood over to hang out. I knew Gary didn't want me having people in the house, and I couldn't bear to think of the disappointed look on his face if he had found out, but I was lonely, and the house was quiet. As time passed, I broke the rules less and less. I stayed up with him in the evenings talking when he came home late and cleaned up so that he could relax when he got there.

I began to save money to send to my children. I took on all the hours I could at the new job, trying to save a little to pay my own way. It was an empowering feeling, not having to depend on anyone else. Gary told me to forget about paying rent when I hesitantly asked him one evening. He wanted me to get on my feet and save some money.

After some time, Gary also convinced me to start studying for my GED. He bought me several books and sat with me late at night, even when I could see he was tired. I worked at all hours. A good situation had finally been thrown my way; I might as well make the best of it before the tide turned again. I wrote to Woode in Missouri and called my step-mother, making awkward small talk to try to reestablish our relationship. I was starting to feel a steadiness I hadn't ever felt before in my life, a sense that I could, perhaps, control what was happening to me.

Gary finally married his high school sweetheart, whom I had met soon after I moved in. She had five kids, and they were all moving in with him. As he explained it, I could see the pain on his face. I told him I understood; I would be out within two weeks. I appreciated all the help he had given me, I explained, and I would be fine with finding a new place to live.

TWENTY-NINE

BUT IT WASN'T FINE. The two weeks was almost up, and I still couldn't find anywhere to go. One day after work, I went to the library to look for apartments on the computer. Discouraged at the high prices, I considered my meager salary and the small amount of savings I had, most of which I had sent to my children.

At the computer next to me was a gigantic white man. He breathed heavily and sipped at a soda, staring at the screen. I looked at him out of the corner of my eye, disgusted despite myself. How could anyone be that fat? He saw me eyeing him, though, and struck up an awkward conversation.

Fat and *stupid*, I thought. This guy actually thought he had a chance with me. But when he asked for my number, for some reason, I gave it to him. It couldn't hurt to have a man on my side when I was about to be homeless.

The next day, he picked me up and we went out to eat. I tried not to stare throughout dinner as he ordered plate after plate. He ate fast, like a pig, breathing heavily through his mouth. It was disgusting to watch him. He invited me back to his grandparents' house, where he lived in the basement. Uneasily, I agreed. It had to be all right if the grandparents were there.

The basement was a pigsty. A dirty smell hung in the air; piles of worn clothing covered the floor. The tables were covered in crumbs and greasy stains. The sink was clogged with hair, and the whole place was dark and dusty. His grandparents were upstairs in the living room, old, frail, and seemingly blind to our presence. An air of neglect hung about the house, even in the upstairs area where they made their home.

On the ratty basement couch, I explained my situation. I was on a mission to find a place to live, and I needed help anywhere I could get it. I could deal with the dirt if I could stay on the couch for a week or two. I told him about the horrible shelter, about my fears about being homeless out in the city. It was cold out, I said, and the streets were dangerous. I waited desperately for him to ask me if I wanted to stay.

But as I was speaking, he reached his heavy arm around my shoulders and leaned in to kiss me. The kiss was disgusting and wet. I nearly recoiled. But my instinct kept me frozen in place. I was on a mission; I needed to do whatever I had to to get a place to stay. It was cold in Minnesota in the winter; the snow was piling up outside, the streets were dangerous, and I'd be dead within days if I had to stay outside. Fighting to keep my nausea from rising, I unbuttoned his pants and had sex with him. I left disgusted and smelling of old cigarettes and dust from the old house. He still hadn't asked me to stay.

THIRTY

WHEN I GOT HOME, I began to call everyone I knew. I couldn't risk waiting on the three-hundred-pound man; I didn't know if it would work, and anyway, I didn't ever want to see him again. I called Terry and my girl-friends, as well as some other people from church, but they had no ideas. Everyone was short on money and didn't have a bed to spare. The only people I knew might have a place for me were my parents, but I couldn't bring myself to call them. The idea of seeing my half brother, and going back into that suffocating atmosphere of shame, was worse than being homeless.

Reluctantly, I called the fat man back the next day and asked if I could stay with him until I could find a place. He told me he'd have to talk to his grandparents. In the meantime, he said wickedly, he'd like to see me again. He picked me up later that day and brought me back to the awful basement. Fighting back my disgust, I slept with him again, hoping it would somehow convince him to let me stay.

He was finally able to convince his grandparents to let me to stay for a week. He said he would help me find a place for after that time. Sadly, I said goodbye to Gary. I was moving in with a new boyfriend, I said; I would be fine. I couldn't help but see the disgust on his face when the fat man pulled up to pick me up with all my things. He asked if I wanted to stay longer, but I said no. He had a family now, and it was time for me to go.

THIRTY-ONE

IT WAS HARD TO SLEEP in the basement because the smell was so bad. I woke up each morning on the ratty couch, disgusted when I remembered where I was. But he had a car and he had a place, and that was better than taking my chances outside.

As the days passed, things became unbearable. The moment I moved in, I refused to sleep anywhere near him. He would whine in the darkness in his bed, asking me to come, and I would pretend to be asleep. I couldn't bring myself to touch him. Finally, we got into a fight.

His face turned red and he spat, "I let you stay here; you should be doing what I want. You don't want to touch me; pack your things and get out."

I was nearly blind with rage. "I'm not going anywhere, you fat piece of shit. You think I wanted to live with someone so disgusting?"

I could see the shock and astonishment spreading across his face. Feeling hysterical and vindicated, I began calling him every name in the book.

"You think I *wanted* to sleep with a slob like you? You think I *like* living in this shithole? This is the dirtiest place I've ever seen in my life.

You know what? Actually, I'll *gladly* move out so I don't have to see your fat face ever again."

With that, I triumphantly swept my hand out and knocked a pile of dirty dishes to the ground. I turned my back, grabbed my purse and a small bag sitting next to the bed, and shoved all the clothing I could into it. As he stood there, shocked, I bounded up the stairs, flew past the blank-eyed grandparents in their chairs, and slammed out the front door.

I called Woode in Missouri collect from the phone in the hotel lobby. I told her what was going on, my momentary high wearing off, and the hysteria beginning to set in.

"I'm staying at a hotel right now. I moved in with this fat piece of scum and I just couldn't do it anymore. I'm going to run out of money and I don't have anywhere to go. I can stay here maybe a couple more days, tops."

She said, "Let me talk to my man and I'll call you back." Two days later, she called to tell me that she had just talked to her father-in-law about me and he had asked her to send him my picture. I should board the next Greyhound bus to Jefferson City, she instructed, and I would stay in Missouri.

"What am I going to do about my job? I barely have any money left."

"Relax. You can stay with us. I'll help you get a job at the warehouse I work at. Plus, get this. My father-in-law is a professor at Lincoln University. He has a big house all to himself, and he likes you. I bet you'd like hooking up with a professor, right?" Her voice was mischievous.

It was exciting. At the same time, it made me nervous to get involved with a well-educated man. I had just recently learned to read. But I'm a girl who can talk to anybody and they'd never know that I was uneducated. I knew if anyone could pull it off, I could. There just remained the question of whether I'd like him.

I called my three-hundred-pound friend and told him I was sorry. I asked if he would please pick me up so I could get the rest of my stuff from his house, then drop me off at the station.

The fat fuck's voice was glowing over the phone. He'd do it, he said in his breathy voice, but I had to have sex with him. I wanted to say no and call the cops to get my stuff from his house. But the Greyhound station was an hour away, and I didn't have the money to take a taxi there. So once again, I'd have to sleep with this man just to get my things and get where I needed to go.

THIRTY-TWO

IT WAS A LONG RIDE on that Greyhound bus from Minneapolis to Missouri.

My girlfriend Woode, her new fiancé, and his friend Kenny picked me up from the Greyhound station. Woode and I hugged, excited to see each other. I couldn't believe the relief I felt at seeing her face after the last few days. There was also another pleasant surprise; Kenny could not take his eyes off me, and I couldn't help but blush. He was a big guy, but he was so damn cute. He had a beautiful smile with dimples in his cheeks. For a big guy he had a soft-spoken voice. His cool sense of style, his walk, and his smile took my breath away.

I was still looking forward to meeting the professor, but the attraction between Kenny and me was instant. The four of us hung out in the apartment, eating, drinking, talking shit about the people I had met in Minneapolis, laughing out loud. As I mopped up some sauce from my plate, Kenny leaned over and handed me a joint. I had never smoked weed before, and as I coughed, he laughed, his eyes sparkling warmly. A sense of peace and relaxation unlike anything I had felt before washed over me. I settled back against the couch, feeling my arms and legs growing heavier, and feeling finally a warm, hopeful feeling growing inside me.

• • •

At six-thirty the next evening, the professor came over. He was an old, ugly-ass Liberian man. I shook his hand, smiling as charmingly as I could, then pulled Woode aside and asked to speak with her in the other room.

I shut the door behind us and said, "You've GOT to be joking. That man has got to be sixty-five years old."

Woode laughed and whispered, "He is very nice. Just give him a chance. He can really take care of you, and then you and I will be related!"

"There is *nothing* about this old man that's appealing. *Nothing.* And I *just* escaped from that fat fuck and I *can't . . .*"

"Why are you being naïve?" she hissed. "This man can help you get on your feet."

So I went with Dr. Waldo to his house, my luggage in tow. I was surprised at how large the house was, with huge windows and a brick front drive. When we got to his house he asked politely if I wanted something to eat. I told him no thanks; I was just tired and wanted to go to bed. He showed me the bathroom. I took a long shower, dreading the conversation when I got out, and then got ready to sleep in the bed he had indicated.

As soon as I got into bed and shut off the light, the door creaked open. I heard him shuffle across the room; I pretended to be asleep, but my heart was pounding, my body tense. He got in the bed with me and started rubbing his body against mine.

"No, please. I'm tired and I need to sleep," I said, trying to make my voice sound tired.

The ugly old man didn't get it. He kept trying to touch me, and I kept protesting that I was tired. After his third attempt, I was overcome with annoyance. I pushed his hand away hard and yelled at him to stop. He finally rolled over silently and left me alone.

At about three in the morning, I awoke to a tug at my legs. I propped myself up and made out a dark shape down at my feet. This ugly-ass professor was trying to pull my underwear down. I sat up, pulled my underwear back up, and shouted "That's it. I'm going to sleep in your living room."

It was all set up, had been handed to me, but I couldn't bring myself to sleep with this man. I wasn't through feeling disgusted about having sex with the fat man, and now I was supposed to sleep with an elderly person? His ugliness and his age weren't the only thing that was disgusting. Even worse was him trying to force himself on me when I didn't want him. He knew my situation and was taking advantage of me. I had had enough.

The next morning, he burst down the stairs and he told me to get my suitcase so he could drop me off at Woode's. I did as he asked with no hesitation. That was the end of that blind date.

THIRTY-THREE

WOODE AND HER FIANCE lived in a one-bedroom apartment in Jefferson City. I slept in the living room. Despite the issues with the father-in-law, which Woode found both frustrating and hysterical, the two were welcoming and warm.

After two weeks in Jefferson City, I got a job as a housekeeper at a Super 8 Motel. I took on all the shifts I could. The work was boring, but it wasn't hard. We scooped up used sheets and towels and dumped them into the carts, scrubbed down bathrooms, and collected the crumpled dollars people left on their nightstands. I was saving money again; I would be able to get my own place soon enough.

After two months, Kenneth and I started seeing each other. Kenneth worked as a security guard at a local business. Things got pretty serious between Kenneth and me.

Finally, we decided to move in together. The first few months were bliss. He was kind and generous, and I couldn't get enough of his smile. We cooked dinner together each night, laughing and joking, inviting Woode and other friends over to visit. He had an old catalog and drove me to work and picked me up each night. He seemed to understand me, and I loved him.

Four months into living together, though, Kenneth lost his job. I was the only person working and paying the bills. I told him I didn't mind covering for him while he found a new one, but three months later, he still hadn't done so. The first time he disappeared, he didn't come back for a week. He came back sweating and looking tired, and when I asked him where he'd been, he snapped at me that it was none of my business.

As time passed, he disappeared more often. He left me stranded at work, and I'd have to walk home in the dark. When I asked him about it, he screamed violently, exasperated. His eyes were beginning to sink into his head now, and he was getting thinner. Was he sick? Had he gone insane? I had no idea what was going on. I desperately wanted the old Kenneth back.

THIRTY-FOUR

ONE DAY, AS I WAS WALKING home from work, a silver Nissan pulled over. An old man said, "What's a beautiful girl like you doing walking on the side of the road?"

I glanced over out the side of my eye and kept on walking.

"Get in, let me give you a ride. Come on. Don't be afraid, I won't hurt you. My name is Eric."

I knew better than to do this, but it was a long walk home and something about his manner made him seem trustworthy. I climbed into the car. Eric took me home politely, and as I got out of the car and thanked him, he gave me his number.

From then on, every time I got stranded I called Eric and he would give me a ride. If he couldn't make it, he would send a friend to help me. He looked to be in his sixties, but he was handsome. He was Nigerian, well-dressed, and his home sounded very nice from the way he described it. He was polite and didn't seem to want anything in return for the rides, so I grew to trust him. I slowly opened up to him on the long car rides, explaining Kenneth's behavior and my growing desperation. Eric told me that Kenneth was doing drugs, an idea that seemed to be reinforced when he started disappearing for three weeks at a time.

One day, Eric picked me up from work and took me to his house to cook for me. I was curious to see his place and see whether he was a good cook. His house was warm and clean, and the meal was delicious. On my next day off, he took me shopping and took me out to dinner.

Eric was old, but young at heart. He was funny, loving, and caring. He genuinely worried about my well-being on my walks home, and he never forgot about me. Before long, we started sleeping together. I kept the secret from Woode, not wanting to tell her that Kenneth's life was unraveling and our relationship was falling apart. One night over dinner, Eric asked me to move in with him.

"You won't pay any bills. You can save up your money for your children. I'll even help you buy a car. Stop living with that lowlife; he doesn't care about anything but drugs."

I considered. It was a no-brainer. I felt warm and safe with Eric, and I was growing increasingly afraid of Kenneth. I went to my apartment, packed all my clothes and shoes, and I was out of there before Kenneth ever came home. Staying with Eric was as great as I had imagined. He cooked dinners and treated me with courtesy every day. He taught me how to drive, laughing as we wheeled around the dead-end streets. Soon after I moved in, he bought me my first car, a gold Honda.

I had my own job and my own car, and I finally felt like I was getting on my feet. I got a second job at a daycare center. I loved being around the children; they reminded me of my own siblings and daughters. I wondered how they looked, how their little voices sounded. I began to ache for them.

THIRTY-FIVE

I DON'T KNOW IF it was the fact that Eric and I had both started working double shifts or the fact that I had my own vehicle, but Eric soon grew paranoid. He would call me ten times in a row while I was at work, leaving voicemails demanding to know where I was. He started complaining any time he arrived home and I wasn't there. On his day off, he'd check to see if I was at work, calling to tell me that he had seen my car somewhere else. He grew jealous and controlling.

Meanwhile, I had applied in secret for low-income housing. When my approval letter came, I moved out of Eric's house into my own. I was still grateful to Eric, and the first few days after I moved out, I returned to sleep with him. He had grown more tender since I moved, sorry for his actions. But I gently explained I was sleeping with someone else. Eric didn't like that, so we stopped seeing each other.

Once I had moved out, I got in touch with the younger side of Jefferson City. It was full off college students, and I began hanging out more with Woode, her newfound friends, and other people I had met in my new housing complex.

I had a lot of friends, but one best friend. Rita was a party animal. She drove a nice car and hung around with the college kids. She knew everyone and everywhere to hang out that was any good. She introduced me to one hot spot, a bar where the music thumped late into the night and drunk boys bought us drinks all night. We began partying every night, meeting new people, laughing and having a blast in the smoke-filled, beer-scented haze of the Jefferson City night scene. We drove around in her nice car for hours, just playing loud music and looking for boys. I was free of Eric, free of Kenneth, free of the parade of men who had tried to control me, free of my parents, free of my past. I howled into the night, the wind rushing in my face, happy in the booming, blossoming spring night air.

THIRTY-SIX

ON FRIDAY NIGHT, RITA AND I went to a popular after-party spot, a gas station called Brake Time. Everyone would get together there after hitting the clubs and hang out. So Rita and I pulled up to the spot after having hit the local clubs hard and headed inside of the gas station to buy a couple of drinks.

As we walked inside, an attractive older guy walked out. He was smooth and charismatic, but his flirtations weren't over the top like so many guys our age. I actually thought he was hitting on Rita; I had never been hit on by a white guy before and thought he was after my white friend.

I brushed him off, thinking he was after her, and we headed inside to get our drinks. I said something to Rita about how he had been pretty interested in her, and she just laughed.

"Uh, no, honey, he was into you," she said. I asked if she was sure, and she laughed, nodding.

"I'll be right back," I said with a saucy twist of my hips.

"Ew! No, don't talk to him. He's old," Rita said, her nose scrunching up.

I rolled my eyes and dismissed her. "Girl, I'll be right back."

I spun on my toes and walked back toward where I'd seen Vince heading. Spotting him quickly, I sauntered up to him and asked how he was doing. He laughed and flashed me a sweet smile.

As we got to talking, he was clear that he was only looking for a booty call. I told him I wasn't looking to just hook up and that if he was interested, he could take me out on a date. He seemed open to the idea, but didn't immediately say yes or no. I gave him my number and went back to hang out with Rita.

Vince called me the next day and asked me out for drinks. I agreed and we had a good time. We had a few drinks and then we spent the night together, his charm having happily lured me into his bed. The next morning, I left early, before he had woken up. I didn't regret what happened, but I was curious if he would prove to still be interested in me, considering that he had only been looking for a hook up.

I was pleased when he called me later that day and asked me out to dinner. It was only our second date, so I was surprised when we pulled up to the fancy restaurant. He had picked me up in a very nice car, so I thought he might have had some money, but I wasn't prepared for how upscale the restaurant was—the kind of place where there aren't prices on the menu. He gave the keys to the valet and I felt out of place before we even walked inside. But I was prideful and held my head high, not letting it bother me.

Confidence is sexy, or so I told myself as we were seated. It did not take long before I was riding the high that comes with wealth and access to nice things. I let my inherent cockiness lead and enjoyed the night. If we were noticed, I'm sure the other patrons thought me underdressed, but I refused to let it get to me.

When I lived with Onike and Steve, I often felt like I was Cinderella living with her wicked stepmother and stepsisters. That night turned my Cinderella story around. Now, I had gone to the ball and had found my prince. And here he was, insisting that he could rescue me from the toil and trouble of my current life. I was more than willing to be rescued. Over the past few years, I had bounced around from place to place, shelter to shelter, sleeping on a friend's sofa one night to renting my own place, as cheaply as possible, the next.

That's when Vince swept into my life with his luxury car, gorgeous home, and what I saw as piles of money to throw away on fancy food. While the money was nice, it wasn't something I was specifically looking for. Ultimately, I wasn't looking for anything at all, not anything serious anyway. I did not particularly want a relationship, but there was something about Vince—and it wasn't his money—that drew me to him. I wasn't hunting for a rich boyfriend, but I wasn't about to turn someone down because of their wealth either. Who would? Plus, even though I'd seen evidence of his money, I was not sure if he was wealthy, living on credit, or just splurging on a date.

People are rarely what they show on the surface. I knew that, but I didn't let it stop me from wanting to get to know him, or anyone else. I was living the single life. My only care was survival, keeping myself on my feet. So if a charming man wanted to take me out, I was more than happy to go and see where it led. Looking back, I'm surprised I didn't have a sense, an inkling of intuition, of the kind of man Vince was. But I didn't. He didn't show his true colors until much later.

At the time, he seemed like a dream come true.

Still, as we sat in that fancy restaurant eating some of the best food I'd ever had, I could not help but wonder what he expected of me, what he wanted in exchange for such a fancy date. There was little in my life that had come for free. As far as I had learned, no one gives someone else something just because. I expected that Vince would want to sleep with me again or that he would hold the fancy dinner over my head for a favor.

He didn't do any of that. Honest surprise rocketed through me when he politely dropped me off at my home after dinner and didn't even push to come inside for a tumble in my bed. Part of his respectful behavior was because of where I lived.

As we casually dated over the next few weeks, I went to his place or we would go out. He never came to my apartment. I didn't exactly blame him either. I was a poor college kid living in low-income housing—the projects, essentially.

When I got up the courage to ask him over, my suspicions were proven right.

"If your place is filthy, I'm not staying," he said.

Unsure of what *filthy* meant in his world, I said he'd be more than welcome to leave if it wasn't up to his standards. I knew I kept a clean house and hoped that he didn't base his expectations on a ridiculous, professional-housekeeper level.

He didn't say a word about the state of my apartment. I think he was somewhat surprised by how tidy and well-kept it was. People have a certain perception of both students and low-income housing, especially when they're paired together. Seeing my place definitely changed how he saw me and how he saw our relationship progressing. He stayed the night, and that was almost a milestone in our fledgling relationship. From that point onward, we were serious. No longer just dating, we agreed to see each other exclusively.

I got my first taste of who Vince really was not long after we became serious. I'll never know why he thought he'd get away with it. Why he thought it would be a good idea to hide his ongoing divorce rather than state it upfront. If he had been forthright and honest about it, I don't think I would have reacted as badly. But as it happened, I was hanging out with Rita one day and she mentioned that her mother knew of Vince. He was relatively well known in the area and Rita's mother had heard that he was still married but separated.

Though angry, I calmly confronted him about it by asking if he was still married. I knew Rita's mother would be right, that he was separated or going through a divorce, but I hoped it wasn't true. For all his faults, Vince was not a man who would lie to your face. If someone asked him a question, he would either tell the truth or dance around it without answering the question at all. He wasn't likely to lie about it; he didn't seem to see the point when the person who confronted him about it likely already knew the truth. At this point, however, I didn't know that about him.

I was surprised when he just said, "Yes, I'm still going through divorce proceedings. My soon-to-be ex-wife is dragging it out."

Later, I would comfort myself with the fact that he was honest about it when I asked him, but this wouldn't be the last time he kept something from me. When I asked him why he hadn't told me, he simply said that I hadn't asked. This too would become a familiar situation. Hurt by his omission and angry that he had hidden it, I broke up with him on the spot. I ended things flat out, not wanting to be the other woman or to be dismissed if he and his ex-wife happened to get back together before the divorce could finalize. Vince seemed to take it fairly well, as we had not been together, or serious, for long. I wouldn't see Vince again for a couple of years, not until after the birth of my son in 2006.

THIRTY-SEVEN

AFTER BREAKING UP WITH VINCE in 2004, I threw myself back into the young party scene in Jefferson City. It was there that I ran into Woode and her boyfriend. We started to hang out again, but our friendship quickly went south.

Woode had never learned to read or write in English, so I would go with her to the store sometimes and help her write checks to pay for her purchases. The night everything went wrong began as a fairly normal encounter; we went into the Walmart, shopped around, and grabbed what we needed. When we got to the checkout line, the cashier rang up the purchases and read out the total. Woode then dug out her checkbook and asked me to fill it out. I did as asked and then passed the fresh check over to the cashier, who entered it in and gave us our receipt. It was as simple and easy as any other transaction.

Except, just a few days later, Woode somehow got it in her head that I was interested in her fiancé. I could not have been less interested in the man, so I'm not sure where she got that idea from, but all she would talk about was how I had been hanging all over him and flirting with him.

I tried to talk to her about it, since my behavior hadn't changed from the first time I met him, but she wouldn't hear me out. Instead, Woode started talking trash about me, and I confronted her about it. There was no way I was going to let it go without asking why she was acting that way, but maybe I should have. The situation escalated, and she started a fight. I'm not one to back down, so I whooped her ass. That wasn't it, though; I let my temper get the best of me. I smashed in her car windows and slashed her tires.

It is not an excuse, but I carried around so much rage, grief, and hurt every day that sometimes it would explode out of me and into the world, a ferocious release of built-up tension and frustration. I would home in on one thing and see red, almost losing control of myself. Never having had a chance to process through every traumatic thing that had happened to me—growing up with an unloving and alcoholic mother, being a child soldier, getting raped by my brother, numerous sexual assaults and unwanted advances—created a pretty pervasive and consistent lack of security and safety. Without knowing how to handle it or how to best care for myself, I carried around a lot of emotional baggage and was not always the best at working through its effects.

When Woode saw what I had done, she went to the police station and filed a report, hoping to get me arrested for check fraud and vandalism. The police brought me down to the station and listened to my side of the story. I stuck to being honest and admitted to what I had done wrong, but insisted that I was not guilty of stealing or check fraud. I don't know what I would have done without the security cameras since it was just my word against hers and I had vandalized her property.

Thankfully, there is not an angle that Walmart doesn't have covered by cameras. The footage from our transaction proved my story, that she had asked me to write the check for her. After the police reviewed the footage, the fraud charges were dropped. The vandalism case, however, stuck. I was charged and fined for vandalism. When that mess wrapped up, I hopped a bus to Minnesota, thinking that I needed a change of pace.

THIRTY-EIGHT

MINNESOTA WAS A WHIRLWIND. I moved in with my parents in 2004, even though it was the last thing I wanted. Still, if I hadn't moved to Minnesota then, I may not have met Richard, Abraham's biological father.

Soon after I found myself settled at my father and stepmother's house, my old friend Jeremiah took me around to try to find a job. When we walked into a group home, I met Richard Ouko, an incredibly handsome soldier in the US Army. We hit it off immediately and our relationship seemed normal. I became a personal care assistant and soon was able to support myself enough to move out of my parents' house and into Richard's. During our romance, he warned me that he would eventually be deployed and that I wouldn't be able to see him for a while. I understood; it was his job after all, not anything to worry about.

We were soon married, and I discovered I was pregnant not long after. The one good thing to come out of my time in Minnesota was my son Abraham. Unlike several of my previous pregnancies, I decided not to have an abortion—I was married and felt like it might be a good time to have a child, a wanted child. When Richard got his deployment orders, I was not overly concerned with how long he would be gone, though I did worry that he would miss the birth of his son. Still, I was not about to complain that my husband had a steady job and my child and I would be provided for while he was away. It seemed a small sacrifice.

Still, while he was away, my personal care assistant job was not enough to pay our bills, so I looked into what could be done to alleviate some of the monetary stress I was feeling. I'm ever thankful that I did this. If I had not, it may have taken me far longer to see through Richard's charade.

I called the Red Cross for financial assistance and explained that I was Mrs. Ouko, Richard's wife, and that I needed to set up financial assistance while he was deployed, as we had a child on the way. It was then I discovered something was off. The customer service person addressed me by the wrong first name and asked why the address I gave was in Minnesota, when the address he had on file was in Seattle. Surprised, I quickly made up a lie about visiting family while he was away, just in case this was not just an error. The customer service person accepted that easily and gave me the contact information for someone who could help me arrange for some of Richard's paycheck to be deposited into my account, but I was far too interested in what, or who, was in Seattle.

A few days later, I packed a bag, bringing my marriage certificate with me, just in case. I was a few months pregnant at this point, but not in an overly obvious way, which I hoped would allow for more civil conversation between Richard, this other woman, and I.

Parking my car in front of a nice suburban Seattle house, I climbed out and headed up the front walkway to knock on the front door. Despite having driven all the way from Minnesota, I did not want to wait. The sooner this was handled, the better, as far as I was concerned.

Despite having my suspicions basically confirmed, there was nothing that could have prepared me for the shock of seeing a nice, well-dressed woman open the door with a confused expression on her face.

Throughout the whole drive, I had no idea what I wanted to say, and a part of me had hoped Richard would open the door and explain that he had never gotten around to telling the army that he had divorced or that his wife had passed away. Maybe it was his religion—he could have been a more traditional Mormon and his wife had no problem with him having another wife. I wasn't happy about that, or any of the other options, but at least those would make more sense than he decided to have two families, without either knowing anything about the other. I threw myself at explanations, desperate to convince myself there was another explanation than what was quickly becoming increasingly obvious.

Unable to make myself tell her the truth on her front stoop in a nice, middle-class neighborhood, I introduced myself as Richard's cousin and said that he had told me to stop by. The woman politely invited me in, saying that Richard was still at work but that he would be home soon, and asked if I would like something to drink. Momentarily, the desire to wait for Richard to come home and make him explain it to her took over, but I stomped on it. She deserved to know, just like I did.

"Ma'am," I began and removed my marriage certificate from my handbag, "I'm not his cousin. I'm actually his wife."

The woman gasped, and I knew she wasn't in on it. She hadn't known any more than I had. She read over our marriage certificate before handing it back to me with shaky hands. She then took a step back, needing the illusion of space.

In for a penny, in for a pound, I figured.

"I'm also pregnant with his child." I kept my voice confident, but gentle.

Richard's first wife fainted. She just froze, looked at me, and collapsed. I did what I could to make her comfortable and helped her come back around. Then we waited, uncomfortable and awkward, for Richard to come home.

The confrontation could have been worse, but ultimately Richard saw the worst of the situation. Our marriage was annulled, having never been valid. Richard received a dishonorable discharge from the army; I'm not sure what happened to him and his first wife.

● ● ●

I drove back to Minnesota and packed my bags, moving out of Richard's and my house. Then, I got back into my Mitsubishi Eclipse and moved back in with my parents. My father and stepmom were having some financial difficulties, which were somewhat helped by my totaling my car the first day after I moved in. I used the insurance money to pay their back mortgage. In return they gave me a fairly new Honda stick shift. I did not know how to drive stick, but I learned quickly. Just a few months later, I found out they had lied to me—the car wasn't mine; they were leasing it. Ripped off and angry, I found somewhere else to live.

Nana had a house and was willing to rent me a room. He started out as my landlord, but we soon progressed to a friends-with-benefits situation. I was still pregnant with Abraham, but it didn't seem to bother him at all. While living with Nana, I also enrolled in cosmetology school, wanting to make more of myself than just being a personal care assistant, but money was tight and there were times I could barely scrape up enough money for gas to drive to school. Still, I persevered as long as I could, knowing that when Abraham was born, I likely would not have enough time, money, or energy to continue going to school.

When I was at my wit's end, I again sought help. This time, I found a local Catholic church that accepted me and offered me help. As far as I was concerned, they were only helping out of pity for me, but I discovered the congregation were lovely, helpful people. While asking for help, I told the priest my story and what had happened with Richard. I may have told a few white lies about my living situation, and I'm not proud of them, but I did what I had to do to survive.

The church opened their arms to me. They helped me to apply for assistance and helped me procure everything a baby might need. They even took me out to eat and grocery shopping occasionally; they also gave me rides to my prenatal appointments when I couldn't make it there myself. Over the months that they helped me, they must have spent hundreds of dollars helping me, and I will always be thankful for their assistance. They were giving and kind, and I don't know how I would have managed without them.

I hid from them that I was seeing Nana at the time, but soon he lost his job and lost his house, so I did not feel as guilty as I might have otherwise. Nana and I were okay, though. He found a place to live, and with the church's help, so did I.

THIRTY-NINE

THE DOCTOR I WAS SEEING during my pregnancy with Abraham was my family doctor, the same doctor I had seen for years. In 2006, my little boy was brought into the world with the help of Dr. Thomas Jones. With the church, Nana, and even some assistance from my parents, I managed to care for Abraham for six months on my own before I became very depressed, even suicidal. Whether it was postpartum depression or simply the effects of single parenthood without much of a support system, I'm not sure, but I felt I had no other choice.

One night, I knowingly took too many pills and wound up in the hospital. I was not there long, which was both a failure on the hospital's on-call psychologist's part and my own. I convinced the doctor that I had taken them by accident and received no treatment for the depression I was drowning in. After they pumped my stomach, they had me evaluated by the psychologist, and he said I wasn't a suicide risk. Then I was allowed to go home.

Around this time, I was still Dr. Thomas Jones's patient. I did not know it was illegal for him to date one of his patients, so when Thomas asked me out after one of our appointments, I said yes. Craving something good, something happy, in my life outside of my baby boy led me not to question much of Thomas's behavior. All I saw and felt was an ever-present gloom; feeling desirable enough to attract a doctor helped me to feel better.

Thomas rented my son and I very nice apartment in Burnsville, and purchased a Nissan Murano in cash—from Vince, incidentally. Baby Abraham and I were quite happy in our apartment, but there was always something a little odd about the doctor's and my relationship.

Sometimes, Nana would watch Abraham while I went out with Thomas, but the doctor and I rarely went out in public together. For a while, I tried to convince myself it was because he was exhausted after his long days in the hospital and simply wanted to relax with me instead of having to deal with the noise and stimulation of a crowded restaurant.

If it ever occurred to me that Thomas might be married, I quickly stifled the idea and did not allow myself to think about it. I did not even find out for sure until after things between us had already gone sour.

FORTY

IN THE FALL OF 2007, while dating Thomas, I returned to Missouri for homecoming. I had left Abraham in Minnesota with my parents and my sister. It was my first real time away from him, but the girls did a good job keeping me from worrying about my son. The girls and I got together to party, and we had a blast. After homecoming, we headed to a club.

It was then that I was convinced fate had stepped in again. From across the room, I spotted Vince. He was lounging in a chair with some other girl on his lap, but I didn't pay her any mind. As far as I could see, she didn't have a ring on her finger, so she didn't matter.

I told my girlfriends, "I'm gonna go get my man back," and they cheered me on as I sauntered across the club. Things had been weird with Thomas, and I knew I wasn't meant to be with him, no matter how nicely he treated me. Something was still peculiar with our relationship, so I didn't hesitate to step right into Vince's space and ask, "Remember me?"

The grin that unfolded across his face was heavenly. His attention completely diverted from the other girl, he said, "I've been looking for you."

We hung out at the club a while longer and then spent the night together in a hotel. Before I left to go home, Vince asked me if there was anything I needed, anything he could do to help me out.

Feeling kind of sassy, I told him that I needed one thousand dollars. He didn't even ask me what I needed the money for; he just pulled out his checkbook and gave me the money.

When he asked, I wasn't sure if he was being real or not, so it was kind of a test. I didn't really expect him to give me the money, but the fact that he did it without question told me that he was on the level, that he really was interested in me and wanted me to be safe and happy.

After that night, I went back home to my son, and over the next few weeks, Vince and I stayed in contact. In November, Vince booked the two of us a vacation to Jamaica. It was heavenly. Our island trip was more than I could have ever dreamed of. The night before we were to return home, Vince told me that he was in love with me. He claimed that I shouldn't be away from him, that he always wanted me by his side.

Shocked, I told him, "I have a son, Vince. I can't just up and leave him behind." I knew that I needed to think about what would be best for my child. Abraham and I were a package deal, and Vince needed to understand that.

Miraculously, he did. He immediately accepted that my son and I were not going to be separated and said that he would welcome him into his home too.

When I went back to Minnesota, Thomas must have suspected that something was wrong. I hadn't told him about Vince, or our vacation, instead saying that I was visiting with girlfriends or similar lies. Similarly, my parents wouldn't hear anything about my being with Vince either.

Vince came to visit me several times in Minnesota, and our love for each other only grew. I distanced myself from Thomas, but hesitated to break it off, as he was my doctor and he was paying for my apartment. I knew I couldn't afford it on my own and did not want to be homeless with my infant son. My parents wouldn't hear of me moving back to Missouri to be with Vince.

One of the times Vince came to visit, Thomas saw the two of us in the grocery store of all places. He became quite upset with me and asked me to move out of the apartment immediately. I agreed to move out, but asked for time to either find a job that would allow me to pay for it myself or to find a new, more affordable place to live. Thomas agreed to my conditions, but we were now on very shaky ground. Things had not been right for a while, and I was becoming quite wary of him. He did not seem to be entirely on the level anymore and I was worried about what he might do—worried enough to set up a surveillance camera in my apartment just in case something did happen.

I've never made a better decision in all my life. One day, when Thomas came by unexpectedly, I turned the hidden camera on and let him in as if nothing was wrong. I caught him up on my job search and thanked him for the time he was giving me to find a new place.

Thomas was acting fidgety and awkward. His out-of-character behavior made me nervous. He pulled out a capped syringe and asked me if I would like to try a new diet drug. As he had been giving me diet pills to help lose the baby weight, this was not as odd as it may sound, but he had never wanted to give me an injection before and it immediately put me on guard.

I turned down the shot, claiming I had lost most of the baby weight and didn't need the diet drugs anymore. Thomas looked very disappointed, so I was happy with myself for listening to my instincts. Thomas left without a fight, but he was almost as unnerved as I was.

One week later, a police detective knocked on my door and said that Thomas claimed I was living in his apartment illegally. I said Dr. Jones and I were in a relationship and that we had recently broken up, that I was looking for a place and had his permission to stay until I found somewhere to live. The detective asked that I come to the station and give a statement. I agreed and provided proof of our relationship, as well as the video of him trying to give me an injection. I waved it off, saying I was his patient too, so him giving me medicine wasn't as odd as it seemed. I was surprised when the detective froze.

She looked at me seriously for a long moment before asking me to clarify that I was a patient of Dr. Jones's. I said that yes, I was Thomas's patient.

Then, crossing her arms and scooting forward in her seat, she asked, "Did you know that it's illegal for a doctor to date their patients, or even treat their family or friends? Those close relationships can compromise their judgment and the quality of care they provide."

Shocked, I said that I didn't know. She recommended I file a complaint against him with the Minnesota medical board, especially considering that he was trying to get me in trouble. The detective also took it upon herself—something for which I am grateful—to inform me that Thomas was also married. I was his mistress and I never even knew it.

I did as the detective suggested, and Thomas was disciplined—a slap on the wrist, but I wouldn't have wanted to ruin his life either. He had to complete a handful of hours of professional ethics training and would be monitored by the board for his compliance. He was allowed to keep his license and continue practicing, provided the required classes were taken and passed.

After six or seven months of dating, Dr. Jones and I were over. We never spoke about it and have actually never spoken since that last time in my apartment.

As I tried to put everything with Thomas behind me, my relationship with Vince was heating up and growing more serious. When I was trying to find somewhere to live after I needed to move out of Thomas's apartment, I wanted to move in with Vince, but my parents were still very against it, especially if I wasn't going to marry him. When I told this to Vince, he proposed. But still, my parents insisted on causing trouble.

When they heard the news, they then insisted on exacting a bride price, a traditional gift the groom pays to the bride's parents to prove his worthiness as a suitor and to repay the bride's family for the loss of her ability to help provide. My parents asked Vince for $50,000 in cash. He paid it, and I moved in with him in Lake Ozark, Missouri, where we were soon married.

FORTY-ONE

LAKE OZARK IS BEAUTIFUL. It's a tourist town, ringed in golf courses, bejeweled with beautiful lakefront homes and restaurants, afloat with spectacular boats. Most of the population of Lake Ozark is white: business owners, retirees, and those who only live there part time, their second home being on the lake. In the summer it turns into a party town, hopping with lakefront bars and live music. It gives the appearance of being a town primarily filled with genuinely wealthy people, but it's not, not completely. Even in the midst of the champagne tasters, there are some with beer-bottle budgets.

Half the population of this tourist town seems to be racist, and almost everyone only hangs out with people of their own status. When my husband first brought me to Lake Ozarks, he took me out to dinner at a restaurant called Ruthie Dee's. Within five minutes, he was sweating so hard that it looked like someone had poured a bucket of water over him. He counted many of the people in the restaurant as friends, but they glared at him as if they didn't know him. I asked him if he'd rather leave. He said firmly that no, he could stay, but I could tell how uncomfortable everyone made him.

I couldn't tell you how many times I got dirty looks when I went out with my husband. Even at the grocery store, people looked at me like I didn't belong. One cashier curiously inquired whether I was there on vacation. I squared my shoulders and said, "Oh no . . . I *live* here," in a proud tone of voice.

My husband owned a car dealership, so I always drove fancy cars. My favorite brands are Mercedes, Lexus, and Jaguar. The looks I got when I drove down the street were incredible. It felt like I was getting pulled over just for driving through the center of town.

The Lake Ozark Police harassed me every chance they get. One of them even claimed I kicked him after I first moved in; I had never seen him before in my life. Let's get something straight: I'm no angel. I can talk my way in with some people, but I have a way of making others not like me. I keep my walls up and my head held high; I have a free spirit and I'm not afraid to speak my mind. Some call it confidence and some call it cockiness, but it all stems from anger and a lack of trust. I don't like when people take advantage of me or of the authority that was given to them; I've seen it happen all my life, and it's nearly ruined my life. And now, in this beautiful lake town, it was rearing its ugly head again. The Lake Ozark Police and I don't see eye to eye.

FORTY-TWO

WHILE MY DIFFICULTIES WITH the police department were as yet unknown, my difficulties with Vince's family were only just making themselves known. Due to my parents' meddling, we had a traditional wedding in Vince's living room. In attendance were my parents, the pastor, Vince's daughter, Amy, and his sister, Mary. All hell broke loose after that day.

To say that his family did not approve of me would be a vast understatement. After we were married, I quickly became the target for Amy's vitriol and anger. If it had only been her, I would have dealt with it better, but the condemnation came down on me from all fronts. Even my husband's sister-in-law Kathy called me a gold-digger and ran a background check on me.

When we went to Kathy's home to visit one day, Kathy demanded to know, in front of the whole family, if Vince knew about the felony her background check into me had turned up. Vince took this in stride, perhaps having expected their intense and protective reaction, as I sat there in tears. He said, "I told Charlesetta that her past is in the past, and everyone has skeletons in their closet."

That woman must have been blessed that day because if it wasn't for her age and my respect for the elderly, I would have cursed her out in her own home before walking off, head held high. As it was, Vince handled it.

For some reason, since the first day I met them, Kathy and her husband Larry have felt the need to play Vince's parents and make it clear that they do not approve of me. They try to play detective, to search out the dark parts of my past and put them on for show. Still, that night was a piece of cake to what I was about to face.

I always thought that after a woman got married, the next logical step would be for her to create a family with her husband. Soon after Vince and I were married, I found out I was pregnant again. I was expecting happy times and excitement, but oh boy, was I wrong. When my husband's family heard about my pregnancy, the door to hell opened wide. But I knew the devil couldn't pull me through the door that easily.

Not long after they found out, my stepdaughter Amy came to me. She didn't even take a moment to think about how I might feel and said rudely, "You need to have an abortion. My dad is too old to have a baby. He'll adopt Abraham instead."

I smiled sweetly. "Well, it looks like your father wasn't too old to fuck a girl younger than his daughter, so I guess he's not too old to have a baby." I watched a look of shock and disgust come over her face.

"My son is looking for a father," I continued. "But I'm not having an abortion. Your daddy told me he was too young when he had you, that he was only sixteen. Now you're saying he's too old to have a child? Somehow I don't think either is true, considering that you're here and so is this baby. You need to stay out of our business." With that, I walked away from her.

Vince's family continued to pressure him based on his age. Finally, he told me to have an abortion or give my baby up for adoption. Shocked, I could barely comprehend what was happening.

He looked at me sternly and said, "If you choose to have that baby, the only thing it will get is child support. It won't have a father." He turned his head away. "I want nothing to do with that baby."

Vince soon filed for divorce. It wouldn't be the last time, even though this time he did not follow through. But he put it in motion and that was that. If he wanted nothing to do with me and our baby, then I wanted nothing to do with him. Between the two of us, it seemed like divorce was always on the table. Over the years, we threatened—both seriously and not—to divorce each other, intending to never see each other again. This time, I knew I was right.

I moved back to Jefferson City and got my own apartment. A few weeks later, just two months into my pregnancy, my husband called me. He had called to say that his youngest sister wanted to adopt my baby. I was speechless and could not think of a worse idea. I outright laughed in his face. It seemed Vince would never stop surprising me.

I couldn't imagine why he had thought his sister and her husband adopting our baby was a good idea. She was married to a man who had been convicted of abusing his children from a previous relationship. Not only was it a terrible idea; it was actually illegal for them to adopt a child, and even if they could, why would Vince want our child to live with them? Everything the Kolb family did showed me how little they thought of me. They must have believed that, as an African woman, my brain was in my ass. How stupid would I have to be to give my baby to a family who not only rejected it before it was born but wanted to send it to live with a family of child abusers?

Vince continued to beg and plead for me to give up the baby and come home. He even traveled to Jefferson City in order to talk to me in person. He must have been hoping to charm me into listening to him, but he didn't have a leg to stand on. One thing he did have was the nerve to stand on my doorstep and tell me that once I gave my baby up for adoption, we could be happy and stay married. He was acting the fool and didn't even know it.

Somehow, he didn't understand what happened between us. It was the first time I realized he needed me more than I needed him.

I looked at his old wrinkled ass and said, "You sound like you think you're the only man for me. Do I seem desperate to stay married to you?"

Vince's face fell. I'll never know whether his reaction was due to shock at my fierce honesty or the realization that I didn't depend on him, that I didn't base my worth on our marriage. In that moment, all the love I had ever felt for him solidified into a deep hatred. He stood in my doorway, speechless and gaping like a fish. It could not have been clearer that my reception wasn't what he had expected when he drove up here intent on winning me back.

I leaned forward and hissed, "Kiss my black ass and *fuck* your family."

Then I slammed the door in his face.

FORTY-THREE

SOMEHOW, VINCE WASN'T DETERRED. He simply didn't stop; he continued to show up at my apartment. The calls from his sister kept coming too. The Kolbs just would not back off no matter what I did or didn't do. Ignoring them worked just about as well as confronting them did, which is to say not at all.

Finally, I couldn't take it anymore. I was afraid for my life. I dropped out of school, packed up my son and everything I owned, and moved back to Minnesota. Four months into my pregnancy, Vince came to Minnesota and begged me to have an American marriage. Between Vince's new promises and the stress of everything that happened, I was convinced.

We went to the courthouse and got a Minnesota marriage certificate. Initially, my pastor wanted to do a traditional wedding ceremony for us. But I explained that we had already had one with my parents and his closest family members according to my culture, and the pastor agreed to marry us without Vince's family present.

I had agreed to the marriage because I thought my husband had a change of heart. That he wanted to make the marriage official to prove to me that he was serious about our baby and about us. After we had our marriage certificate, I went back to Missouri for the wedding.

After months of stress and fighting, things suddenly seemed normal again. He was sweet and caring; he took me on late-night walks when my back hurt, bought me every snack I wanted, and returned to being the kind man I had met years ago. I was a little paranoid about taking the risk that he might go back to being nasty, but I was happy he wanted to be part of the pregnancy. Maybe part of me longed for my children to have a father; maybe I felt like I owed my son and my unborn baby what I didn't have growing up.

Before I knew it, I was being pressured to sign a postnuptial agreement saying that all of his property would go to Amy rather than my children and me when he died. I refused to sign it. It wasn't that I felt entitled to everything that was his or that I didn't want Amy to have anything. I just wanted my fair share for myself and my children. My refusal did not go over well.

When I said I wouldn't sign it, my husband did a one-eighty on me. He went from being a sweet, caring man to someone who, once again, wanted nothing to do with me. He screamed and yelled; I held fast in my refusal. Vince gave me the silent treatment, glaring at me and refusing to speak.

Then, one morning, I woke up and headed out to my doctor's office for a prenatal checkup only to find out that my brake line had been cut.

It was the last straw. I wouldn't endanger my son, my unborn baby, or myself by staying around Vince and his dangerously crazy family. Without hesitating for even a second, I reported the incident to the police and explained what was going on in my home. Then I boarded a bus and left Missouri.

I had a two-year-old, no money, and I was pregnant. I had gone from a lakefront home into a shelter. I was too ashamed to go home to my family and friends. Everybody thought I was married and living comfortably; I couldn't bear to let them down or move back into a shelter. I had come too far to start over. So much for my Cinderella ending; I had sincerely believed this man to be my saving grace, the white knight who would sweep me off my feet and save me from all my problems. Instead, Vince only caused strife.

FORTY-FOUR

AT SIX MONTHS PREGNANT AND DESPERATE, I called my husband and asked him for money to fix the car. He asked where I was, and I told him the name of the shelter where I was living.

"Why are you in a shelter?" he asked, sounding astonished.

"Where else did you think I'd be?" I asked bitterly. "I didn't have the money to rent a place, and I'm too ashamed to go home."

My husband asked to speak to the shelter director, and I handed the phone over to her. I heard his voice through the receiver as he told her that it was my fault I was there; all I had to do was sign an agreement and I could come home. I realized, horrified, that he was trying to get her to kick me out. I motioned to her to give the phone back to me.

His voice was angry. "Just sign the postnuptial agreement and I'll send you some money."

I refused again, stronger this time, and lowered the receiver.

The shelter director leaned over and said, "You can stay long as you want. There a lot of programs that can help you get on your feet. Don't sign the agreement."

After a month and a half in the shelter, I had had enough. I called my friend Makoya, explained the situation, and asked if my son and I could come stay with her.

She agreed, and my son and I made the two-and-a-half-hour drive to Coon Rapids, Minnesota. Makoya had separated from her abusive husband, so she understood where I was coming from and what I might be needing. She had three kids of her own and very little income from her CAN job, but still she helped me. She couldn't afford her mortgage but agreed to let me stay with her if I went to the state for assistance. I was approved for food stamps and cash assistance, receiving about $500 in stamps and $437 in cash to get me through. I finally felt good, like I might just be able to get back on my feet. Even though I was on assistance, it was a point of pride that I was able to help my girlfriend with food and some cash.

Even though Makoya did her best, the house was very uncomfortable. It was falling apart and full of cockroaches. The heat didn't work, and it was freezing. I thought living with my friend who at least had her own place would be better than the shelter, but I was wrong.

More nights than I can remember, I stayed up and checked on my son every hour. Between the cold and the bugs, I was terrified that something would happen to him. Maybe a cockroach would crawl into his ear or mouth, maybe the cold would prove to be too much and he would get hypothermia. It was worse than the shelter; I had to get out.

The one thing that Makoya's home did provide was time. While living there, I was able to save enough money to get my son and I a one-bedroom apartment. It was in a rough neighborhood, filled with drug dealers and other shady-looking characters, but I was happy. I wasn't living on someone else's charity. The apartment was in my name. It was clean and Abraham was comfortable. When I sprung the news on Makoya, she got angry at me for not giving her enough notice. I apologized, but it spiraled out of control. This caused our falling out and we never spoke again.

FORTY-FIVE

A FEW MONTHS AFTER MOVING OUT, on February 19, 2010, I had my daughter. I was in labor for two days before they took me into surgery. I named her Vincetta Onike Kolb. After her birth, my stepmother called Vince in Missouri to let him know he had a daughter.

Vince and his sister who wanted to adopt my baby drove to Minnesota a week later to meet her. It was both terrible and relieving to see him there. I still held out some hope that he would love her. The first time he held her, tears came to his eyes. I asked him bitterly if they were tears of joy or tears of guilt.

When his sister reached for the baby, he told her sharply to back away. My parents and I were at a loss for words. After they left, my stepmother, a nurse, said drily that she wouldn't be surprised if both Vince and his sister had bipolar disorder. I couldn't find it in myself to disagree.

Vince called the next day and asked me to have a DNA test done to prove the baby was his. I agreed, knowing she was his, so he gave me instructions to the medical office where I could have it done. On the day of the test, I was sick to my stomach. I didn't understand why this man was still hurting me, why he was trying to disgrace me in front of my family. It was a nightmare that I couldn't wake up from. A nightmare that I had to relive over and over, waiting for it to end, but never seeing the light at the end of the tunnel.

This time, I made sure to look at the test results myself. Of course, they came back saying that he was the father. After he received the results of the paternity test, he asked me to bring Vincetta to Missouri so that his family could meet her. Not wanting to keep him from his daughter entirely, I agreed.

When we got to Missouri, my husband put me up in a hotel and took my baby home with him, leaving me there alone. I had a bad feeling, but once again, I gave him his way. I was so afraid to bring another baby into the world without a father. I wanted him to be involved. I was scared, but I took the chance.

I took a lot of chances in life.

FORTY-SIX

AS SOON AS THE BABY and I returned to Minnesota, my husband called and said he didn't want a divorce. He wanted his family. He begged me to move back to Missouri and be his wife. He promised to protect and love my children and me. He even promised to open a clothing store for me. He knew it had always been my dream to own a boutique.

"Consider it a gift," he said, "for all the pain and disgrace my family and I have caused you."

Vince seemed genuine and honest, more than he had ever been before, so I accepted his heartfelt apology. It didn't hurt that I was suffering too. No matter what he had done, life without him was awful, and I knew life would be easier in many ways, if not always pleasant, with him in it.

I wanted my children to have a father, and most importantly, I didn't want to raise them in a shelter, struggling to survive. The decision was easier to make than I thought it would be. Once again, I gave up my furniture and my apartment and left my family and friends. Vince sent me some money for the move, so I packed my kids and all our belongings into a U-Haul truck, hitched my car to the tow dolly, and drove the ten long hours to Missouri. As scared as I was to move back in with Vince, I was hopeful too.

For the first six months, everything went smoothly. He kept his promise and opened the store for me on a side street in downtown Lake Ozark. I had a live-in nanny for my baby and we were well provided for, even if he didn't keep his promise to protect me. But I wasn't worried; I have always been a fighter. From the moment I was conceived until my dying day, I think I will always fight. I'm not sure I know how to do anything else when fighting might be necessary.

FORTY-SEVEN

AFTER OPENING MY STORE ONE MORNING, I decided to take a break and go home to clean the house. While going through some of my husband's things, I ran across some provocative pictures of Vince's ex-girlfriends. I weighed the evidence, debating whether I should say something and cause a fight or just get rid of them. I decided to burn them all and leave the ashes in the sink as a sign that I had found the pictures and wouldn't tolerate them.

Amy must have heard about what I had done or seen the unburned shreds, the curled edges with women's faces and hair peeking off the scraps of paper. Regardless of how she found out, Amy assumed I had burned pictures of her stepmother, who had passed away years earlier, rather than provocative photos that her father had kept of old girlfriends. The next day, after I had just gotten out of the shower, there was a knock on my bedroom door. I grabbed my robe and saw Amy standing there.

Without warning, she got in my face and said, "I'm going to whoop your ass."

"Excuse me?" I said, staring her down.

Amy stood taller than my five feet and was probably two hundred pounds compared to my one hundred fifteen. It didn't matter. I made up the difference with the pure anger in my stare.

She said, "You heard me, bitch."

I smiled. I've always found it's good to react in strange ways to aggressive people; it intimidates them. A confused look crept across her face, then she took a step back and slapped me.

From there on, all I saw was red. I pulled her outside, out of sight of my children, and beat the shit out of her. She underestimated my size and thought she could kick my ass; I kicked hers like the stepchild she was.

I got dressed for work and stopped by my husband's office. I stalked through the door and said, "Your daughter just attacked me in my home. You tell *her* that the next time she comes to *my house* to attack *me*, she won't be leaving alive."

Vince stared at me, then calmly asked me to leave his office. I refused.

"What did you tell your daughter? She wasn't there when I burned those pictures. And what the hell were you doing keeping those old pictures anyway?"

He became flustered and upset. He barked that if I didn't leave, he'd call the cops on me. Well, that was putting gas on a fire. I started cussing him out, screaming, all the anger from the previous months erupting out of my body like a volcano. I had moved here for him, and he and his disgusting family weren't going to ruin my life again. He called the cops and tried to force me out himself, but I hung on to the desk.

When the cops arrived, I told them I wasn't leaving. Next thing I knew, I felt the cold metal snap of handcuffs being put on me from behind. My wrists were so small that the cuffs couldn't hold me, so I wiggled out of them; and instead of zip-tying me, they tried to manhandle me. I fought back.

Suddenly, my face erupted in fire. I couldn't see anything; everything went black. I wheezed and felt like I was going to vomit. I had been pepper-sprayed; finally, the Lake Ozark Police had gotten a chance to do what they always wanted to me. All I could hear was them shouting at my husband to get back as I writhed on the floor.

They loaded me into the back of the police car, brought me to the station, and booked me. I couldn't see, but I kept begging the cops to cover me up. I could feel that my dress had slipped down and my breast was exposed. They stood over me laughing, and finally, after twenty minutes, one officer took me in the bathroom to help me wash my face and fix my clothes.

This was police brutality, plain and simple. I was manhandled and disrespected, all because one cop claimed I kicked him. Then the entire force was against me. Even if I had kicked him with menace and purpose, I am not a large person—I am short and was very thin at this time. Police officers are trained to subdue criminals. Were the police seriously threatened by me? Threatened to the point where pepper spray, humiliation, and manhandling that left me seriously bruised were necessary? I just don't think that they acted with the care and training indicative of their position.

FORTY-EIGHT

BEFORE I KNEW IT, I was being charged with third-degree assault on a police officer. As black as I am, I had bruises to prove that these officers assaulted me; none of them had any bruises. But supposedly I had kicked them and beaten them up. I was locked up for twenty-four hours on $50,000 bail.

While waiting for my day in court, Vince's sister called to let me know that Amy didn't want me at her wedding. Vince had told her that I was his wife and he wanted me there, but his daughter had gone to her aunts and uncles to plead her case. I had had no intention of attending her wedding from the start but was willing to go if he wanted me there. The family told him that it was her day and it would be nice if he kept me away.

I told Vince it was fine if she just wanted him at the wedding, but I soon realized she was still working to drive us apart. The day of her wedding, she booked him a hotel fifteen minutes from our home, and neither she nor Vince called to let me know he would be staying there.

My husband asked his friend Brian Burke, an attorney, to represent me in court. The day of my hearing, the prosecuting attorney offered a plea deal. It involved three years of unsupervised probation, a fine, and anger management classes I'd have to pay for myself. This would make my sentence a misdemeanor and not a felony. I refused to take it; I wanted to go to trial. I wasn't going to give these cops the satisfaction of admitting I had done anything wrong.

Brian leaned in and said, "Look around you. Do you think a white jury is going to go against a white cop? If you're found guilty, you'll get five to ten years in prison. You'd better accept the plea deal."

I did.

Have you heard the saying, "You mess with one police officer, you mess with them all"? In this little town, I had been marked with bruises on my body and as a target by the entire police force.

FORTY-NINE

MY HUSBAND LEFT EARLY ONE MORNING several weeks later for an auction. I went to his office to get our daughter's birth certificate. While looking through his files, I came across a postnuptial agreement. My blood ran cold when I saw that my husband had forged my signature on the bottom. Numb and angry, I went straight to the Jefferson City Police Department and filed a complaint. They told me that they couldn't take any action, as he was my husband, but they'd keep my complaint on file. I stood there, stunned and angry.

The officer leaned forward and suggested, "If it's really a problem, go see the secretary of state and file a complaint against the notary." I went straight to talk with a divorce attorney and filed for divorce, then went home and waited silently on the couch for Vince to arrive.

When he came in the door, I confronted him about the forged agreement. I told him I was filing for divorce and was going to file a complaint against his friend who had notarized the agreement. I spat that I had evidence that I hadn't signed the agreement; I was on record as being in the shelter during the time I had supposedly signed it.

He began apologizing and telling me he loved me. He begged me not to file a complaint against his friend and promised to destroy the forged agreement. Now, I didn't trust my husband to begin with, and he had just lost all my respect and love. I had been holding onto my marriage because of the fear of being a single mother raising four children alone. I was also afraid of losing the lifestyle I had grown accustomed to. Without all the bad in my husband, I still saw a man who had a heart of gold.

My family and friends told me to divorce him, but they weren't in my shoes. They couldn't understand. I also knew that none of them would help us, my children and I, if I were to leave Vince.

Who are we if we don't forgive? I truly did forgive my husband and his family. But I didn't trust them. I had no trust in my marriage, my surroundings, or my husband's family. I kept my walls very high around Vince and his family, especially his daughter.

FIFTY

AFTER MY THREATS OF DIVORCE, Amy came over to speak to me. She said bitterly, "What are you doing? That man who notarized the agreement has been a good friend of my family all my life. If you're really in love with my dad, why does it matter if there's a postnuptial agreement?"

"This is none of your business," I said.

Her nostrils flared. "You're nothing but a high-priced prostitute and a gold-digging bitch."

I said sweetly, "Thanks for knowing my worth." I smiled, then continued, "You're a gold-digging bitch of a daughter. You wouldn't have shit without your father. You've had two businesses that your daddy and granddaddy opened *for* you, and they didn't go anywhere. You still have to work for your father. You know why? Because you were a drug addict just like your mother, who fucked your daddy's best friend in his bed."

"Fuck you, you nasty whore." Her lips twisted into a hateful grin. "My daddy told me that you had a baby with your brother." With that last dig, she turned on her heel, climbed into her car, and left.

I couldn't let it go. The next day, I visited their office to defend myself against the world for something I never wanted and hadn't asked for.

"I didn't have a baby with my brother. I was raped by my half brother, and it wasn't my fault."

"This is a place of business," Amy said, looking stunned. "Get out."

I said, "You're just mad because you married a convict and you've never done anything with your life. You're mad because you made nothing of your life. I came up from the bottom and you've thrown away everything you've ever had. You're mad because I made a better choice by marrying your daddy." I walked out the door, got into my Mercedes, and sped out of the parking lot.

FIFTY-ONE

OVER THE NEXT FEW YEARS, things between Vince and I did not improve. We fought, we made up, and it all repeated. Around Christmastime in 2013, we went on a family trip. I can't say visiting Branson, Missouri, was a vacation, even though it was supposed to be. The trip was nothing but torture.

Every day we were gone, the children and I did only what my husband wanted us to do. We did not have a say in what was going on. Not only that, but throughout the vacation, Vince became steadily more abusive. On December 27, 2013, my husband took me to the emergency room because he had reinjured my left arm earlier that evening.

When we were finally seen to, he told me to lie to the doctor. He wanted me to say that I had hurt it while we were just playing around, wrestling and having fun. That it was an accident. I did lie and I did it to protect him, but it was still somewhat out of ignorance. As far as I was concerned, Vince hurt me because he was stressed by work and by his family and because he drank.

Whether or not the doctor believed me, I'm not sure, but the following day was Vince's family Christmas party. No matter how long I had been with Vince, his family never grew to like me. Instead, they chose to always believe the worst of me.

That year, I was somewhat thankful that I would not be going to the party with Vince and the children, as I had spent the evening in the emergency room. I still had to cover my injury as best as I could, however, because Vince had hired a photographer, Henrietta, to come over and take a family picture of us. Before she arrived, I prepared myself and got the children ready for the party too.

When Henrietta arrived and got her equipment set up, she had us pose together in several different ways and snapped a bunch of pictures. My face hurt from putting on a fake smile for so long. Soon, the photographer left and then my husband and children took off for the family party. Little did I know that it would create the biggest fight within the Kolb family that I had ever been a part of.

The next morning, Vincetta showed me what her half-sister Amy had given her as a Christmas present, an American Girl doll called Addy Walker and the accompanying book that told her story. At first the doll and book seemed like a nice gift for my three-year-old daughter, but once I read the book, I became very upset. No matter how beautiful the doll was, the book was completely inappropriate for a three-year-old.

The book talked about Addy's years as a slave during the end of the Civil War. The girl's family had been planning an escape when their master decided to sell some members of her family before they could leave. Now, since the book came with the doll, I understand that not giving the book to us would have seemed odd, but I wish Amy had talked to me first.

I did not want my three-year-old reading about slavery, especially not a little girl who was born a slave. She was too little to understand. As far as I'm concerned, talking about important things, like slavery and racism, should be handled by the parents and it is up to the parents when they approach the topics. It was not Amy's place to initiate that conversation. If she had just given Vincetta the doll and then sent the book home with Vince, so we could decide when to give it to Vincetta, that would have been more than fine. The doll was a lovely gift and I was thankful that Vincetta had such a nice doll.

Since I did not want to cause unnecessary trouble, I asked Vince to read it too and tell me what he thought. He refused to even look at it. Instead, he said that he did not want me to start any more drama with his daughter.

Feeling frustrated, but rather than push the issue with him, I talked to three of my girlfriends—all of them white—and asked them to read the book. They did and immediately said that they would never give the book to a three-year-old, especially not one from a black family. My friends thought the doll was lovely, but everyone agreed the book should have been given to Vince or me separately because of the sensitivity of the topic. I firmly believe that it is up to the parents when and how their children learn about sensitive parts of history, like slavery, provided they are taught the facts at age-appropriate times.

I completely agreed, especially since Amy was white too. Initially, I was not sure if Amy was trying to say something or just wanted to give Vincetta a nice gift. Given my friends' quick and shocked reactions, I felt confident that I had not been overreacting about the book.

I contacted Amy and very nicely thanked her for the gifts, but asked what her intention was when giving Vincetta the book. I only wanted to know why she'd chosen that doll for my daughter so I could explain my hesitations in a way that wouldn't cause Amy to overreact. Obviously, that did not work.

Originally, I thought Amy might have said, "Oh, I just thought she'd like to have a doll that looks like her," or "I know a lot of kids love American Girl dolls, so I thought she'd like to have one."

Instead, Amy skipped right over any polite response and immediately spat, "Fuck off," and hung up on me.

Angered and shocked, I called her back and said, "Fuck you!" before hanging up on her.

This was not the first time Amy and I had gotten into an argument on the phone, so I genuinely thought that was it, that there would just be uncomfortable silence between the two of us next time we saw each other, which was hardly unusual. I was surprised when Amy called Vince a few minutes later and said that I had called her a racist. She went on to whine that she was very hurt by my insinuations and that she was utterly destroyed by what I had said to her. When he got off the phone, Vince told me that Amy said she felt sorry for him, sorry that he was saddled with such a nasty person for a wife. Since Vince had not read the book, he wasn't aware of what I had seen. So when Amy insisted that she went out of her way to make my children happy and that in return she only received horrifying accusations, Vince had no reason not to believe his daughter over me, despite the fact that I was his wife.

I tried to explain to Vince what had upset me and why, but he would not listen to me. He virtually ignored me, my points, and my own feelings about the situation. Instead of taking my perception into account, instead of considering me worth paying attention to, he continued to go on about Amy.

For some reason, she thought that the fact that the doll was expensive should more than make up for the book, especially since I might want to read it to Vincetta when she is older. Amy claimed that if I found it offensive, all I had to do was not read it to Vincetta. Her biggest problem, she explained to Vince, was that I had called her a racist, which was completely unfounded and out of line. It was also completely and utterly false.

As for her accusations, I'm not sure where she came up with the idea that I called her racist, since the word never left my mouth. Amy told her father and anyone who would listen that I had gone on a tirade, berating her for being a racist and giving my daughter an offensive book, which she claimed she hadn't done—or at least not on purpose, as I so clearly said she did. This was not the first or last time Amy made something up to suit her own purposes, her own interpretation of a situation to better serve herself and her point. Amy's idea of the truth was rarely that. Instead, she favored an emotional interpretation that may not have had any basis in reality outside of her own feelings.

In reality, none of what she said had happened. Only Amy knows where most of this story came from, since her lengthy diatribe to Vince was nowhere near the situation that had happened on the phone between us. Regardless of the actual events of that evening, that Sunday became very nasty between my husband and I. I still remember just how angry I was, how Vince's reaction made me feel powerless, like I didn't matter as much as his daughter.

Vince was enraged at my supposed behavior, that I dared to speak that way about his daughter. He berated me for calling her names and thinking that she had anything but the best intentions when giving gifts to my children. He became so upset that he took an ice cold bucket of water and dumped it over my head, right in front of the children.

He had been screaming and yelling, which wasn't entirely unusual, but any sort of physical act of violence had usually been kept fairly private. The children had not seen much, if anything, at this point. Scared that he would lash out and either hurt me more in front of them or that he would hurt them, I called 911.

When the police arrived, it did not go the way I thought it would. The officers at the scene wanted me to write a police report indicating my husband's abuse, saying that I had medical records to back up my claim. While that may have been the right choice in the long run, I was terrified and naïve. Still somewhat convinced that Vince did not really want to hurt me, I wanted to get away from him, but I did not really want to hurt him because I thought he hit me because I deserved it. I had angered him on top of the stress and his drinking, which caused him to lash out. Now I know that this is simply not true. It was not my fault that he beat me.

Vince was a local business man, and having a police report filed against him, especially if I left him at the same time, would obviously cause trouble for him within the community. While I may not have liked Vince very much, I loved him and wanted nothing to do with publicly calling him out on his abuse. Even the few police officers who did want to help me could not do much without a written statement, let alone the officers who seemed to think that I was getting what I deserved.

The officers at my door wouldn't take no for an answer and demanded that I write a statement before they would do anything. I continued to refuse until one of the officers grew exasperated and asked why I wouldn't. Seeing an opportunity to get out of the conversation without having to anger the police further, I claimed that I couldn't write in English. Having no other option, the officers asked that one of us leave the house for the night and that we try to reconcile another day.

This whole situation would not have been particularly noteworthy except that just two days later, on New Year's Eve, Vince went behind my back and filed a police report against me. This led to my arrest that evening. It was a complete shock. He had not given me any warning or sign of what he had done or why. I just opened the door when the police arrived, and they arrested me, charging me with assault with a deadly weapon. The court then ordered me not to return to my home for thirty days.

FIFTY-TWO

FOR THE FIRST FIVE DAYS of 2014, I was homeless. Then I rented a vacation house a block away from home, so my children were able to move in with me and still catch their regular bus to school. Right on the heels of my arrest, I was served a restraining order on behalf of Amy Kolb.

Throughout January, my husband did not seem to understand what he had done to me, let alone to our relationship. He repeatedly called me and left me messages saying how much he missed me, how much he wanted me back. At the time, I did not know how familiar his behavior would sound to thousands of other women and victims of abuse. This was his typical cycle, though it usually did not go to such extremes. He would hit me, leaving bruises and sometimes resulting in trips to the emergency room. Then he would be apologetic and kind, as if nothing had happened, while simultaneously promising that it would not happen again. But it inevitably would. Whether I would anger him or he would go off on one tangent or another, we always circled back around.

One way in which this situation was different was my hesitancy to be a part of it because of Amy's restraining order. On January 25, 2014, Vince came to my rental house pretending to be sick and begged me to take care of him. Even though I was still very upset about the restraining order and how I had been treated, I did not feel like I could turn away my ill husband, no matter what his daughter had done or how he had reacted.

I allowed him into my home and got him settled before heading to the store for some cold and flu medication to ease his complaints and lower the fever he claimed to have. When I returned, I offered him the medication, which he said he would take later, and made him some soup. Vince was the perfect patient while we ate dinner. As soon as we finished our food, it was like a switch flipped. The next thing I knew, Vince had taken me to my bed and pushed his head between my thighs.

I told him to stop, that I didn't want to have sex with him. But he didn't stop, and I gave in. His attentiveness was enjoyable, even though I was upset about what had happened and about him clearly faking sick just to get back into my life. He thoroughly distracted me, reminding me of the trip we had taken to Jamaica years ago—the passion, devotion, and phenomenal sex.

Still, none of this changed how I felt about what he had done or what had happened between us. I didn't think there would be anything that could make up for his calling the cops on me, especially not when I had not been the violent one. Vince had hit me and injured me numerous times, but then he is the one who files a police report and gets me arrested for assault with a deadly weapon? There was no amount of amazingly good sex that could make up for his cruel and repulsive behavior or his history of treating me like dirt.

As we laid cuddled together in the darkness, he told me about Amy's medical troubles. She had had plastic surgery not long before, a tummy tuck, and was experiencing some complications. Vince said that there was something wrong, that she couldn't seem to stop bleeding and that it was pretty bad. Even though Amy and I did not get along at all, I was worried for her. Before he returned to our home, he promised me that he would speak with Amy and arrange to have the charges and restraining order she had filed against me dropped.

It was a big, fat lie.

• • •

It wasn't until the first week of February 2014 that I moved back home, just a handful of days before my thirty-third birthday. From almost the first moment I set foot back in that house, everything started to crumble under me. Vince went from seeking out my attention and demanding that I take care of him and have sex with him to screaming verbal abuse at me in front of my children and threatening to have me murdered.

Not one to sit down and take it, I gave it back as good as I got it, but I was terrified for my children and myself. Though I did not think that Vince would hurt the kids, it was not good or healthy for them to hear their father screaming that their mother was a "cunt" and a "nigger," especially when my son is black and my daughter is mixed. What really terrified me, though, were the threats of murder.

Vince's first wife had been murdered. After she and Vince had divorced, and she took nearly everything he had, his ex-wife was murdered by a man the Lake Ozark police claimed was her "crackhead boyfriend." Something about that never sat right with me. She had been an upper-class white woman living the high life—why would she have a crackhead for a boyfriend? It wasn't until Vince started to threaten to have me killed that I contemplated what might have actually happened to his ex-wife.

Now, I'm not accusing Vince of murder. I'm only illustrating what was going through my mind when he was threatening me. I believed he would have me killed. As far as I was concerned, he was perfectly capable of hiring a hit man. It was not like the Lake Ozark Police would look very hard for me if I went missing or spend too many man-hours searching for my murderer should the worst happen.

Our daily arguments had the police in and out of our residence on a nearly daily basis. One time, Vince called the cops and claimed that I had threatened to kill him with a knife. They arrived and arrested me, despite their being no evidence of me having done anything of the sort—and I hadn't. They charged me with *assault with a deadly weapon* when I hadn't threatened to kill Vince at all, unlike how he continually attacked and threatened me.

Once arrested, I was offered a plea deal, but since they had nothing against me—it was literally just he said / she said—I told my attorney that I would take my chance with a trial. There was nothing to convict me on, and I trusted the justice system at least that much.

Immediately after hearing my response to their offer, they dropped my charge to *disturbing the peace*, a far lesser charge that carried no jail time. They thought they could get me on that in court when they knew they had nothing to prove assault. I was then released on my own recognizance until the date of the trial, but the trial never happened. It was held over my head for two years, until 2016 when Vince and my divorce was finalized.

Once the divorce went through, they dropped all charges. Vince had refused to testify against me when the police asked him to, and rightfully so, as it was Vince's fault I was in the mess to begin with. Without his testimony or any physical evidence, they had no case and the charges were dropped.

The only reason the charges hung around that long was because Vince and his buddies wanted to make sure they had something on me to make sure I wouldn't fleece him when we got divorced like his ex-wife had. As long as I received enough to provide for my children and myself, I was content to take less than I may have deserved in the divorce; I wasn't eager to be the second Mrs. Kolb to be murdered. Barely a week later, Vince reported me to the FBI and said that I was bringing children into the United States for prostitution.

Yes, you read that right.

My husband called the Feds on me and said I was participating in human trafficking. The FBI came to our house in the middle of the night, arrested me, and took me to jail. I spent four hours sitting in jail before being seen by the judge first thing in the morning. A psychiatrist came to talk to me before going before the judge, and I explained what had happened. I was terrified that they would actually believe what Vince had said about me. I would never have brought children into this country to be used as prostitutes.

The very idea sickened me, especially considering the only person I brought here was my own daughter, the product of incestuous rape, and my own history of being a child soldier. After hearing my explanation of what happened, the psychiatrist told me to just tell the judge the truth, so I did. I told the judge that Vince was trying to discredit and hurt me because of our disintegrating marriage; he wanted me deported. Vince hoped to divorce me and get custody of Vincetta so he would not have to pay child support.

See, this all started the previous summer when I brought my eldest child, Sia, into the United States. Sia is a United States citizen, but she did not have a US passport, and our relatives in Africa refused to help her apply for one so she could come live with me. I filled out the documents with all of her information, but she was in Ghana, and without the help of our family, she could not get a passport photo taken. Without that photo, she would not be able to come to the United States.

A friend of mine had a daughter who was just about Sia's age, sixteen, and the two girls looked remarkably similar, so my friend allowed me to use her daughter's photo so I could get Sia into the country. It worked; my daughter came to the United States and was immediately enrolled in school.

Sia took to life in the United States easily. Everything went off without a hitch until Vince decided to report me.

After admitting to the judge that I falsified government documents and lied on a government application, I apologized for breaking the law. I was sorry too. I did not want to cause any trouble or lie; I had no malicious intent to commit fraud. I did not even know it was a crime! Sia was a US citizen and all her information was accurate; the only aspect of the passport that wasn't was the picture. It was a decision made from desperation, as I hadn't seen or held my child in sixteen years. The judge asked why it had been so long since I had seen her, and suddenly the explanation of Sia's conception was relevant. I told the judge what had happened to me when I was my daughter's age and how my family had reacted.

Part of the reason I wanted to bring Sia to the United States in the first place was to have a DNA test run to prove to my family what my brother had done to me. I thought having a DNA test to prove paternity would help. Crying in front of the judge, I said I had never blamed Sia for her father's actions, and though she did not know of her paternity at the time, I did not want her to ever think I blamed her for her father's sins.

After checking my criminal record and assessing my flight risk, the judge released me on supervised probation until trial. This was in 2014. Over two years later, as of the writing of this book, the trial date is still pending. I check in with my probation officer weekly and receive regular drug tests. Being on supervisory probation is invasive and unnecessary given the circumstances and considering I have been denied due process. The only thing I learned from this experience is that when Vince decides to make trouble, he dedicates himself to it.

● ● ●

When Sia was sixteen, I brought her back to the United States to live with Vince and I. Even though Sia and I didn't know each other and our relationship was awkward, we were making it work. She consistently asked me who her father was because my auntie had told her that he had died. My family was too ashamed to tell her the truth of how she had been conceived, if they even believed it, so we kept her paternity a secret.

In December of 2014, after we had started divorce proceedings but before my children and I moved out, Vince told Sia the truth about her paternity. He told her that my own brother was her father and said she was the product of incest. Angry with me for our divorce, he took it out on Sia. He followed her around the house, demanding if she knew who her father was.

Then, one day, he couldn't take it anymore and he spat, "Did you know you were conceived through incest? Your uncle is your father."

Shocked and scared, Sia turned to me and asked, "Mommy, is that true?"

I had no choice but to say yes. There was no way that I could lie to her about something so important. She deserved to know the truth; I was just waiting for the right time. I was waiting until I knew her, until she would trust me enough to hear me out. I was waiting until she was mature enough to understand that it is never a rape victim's fault that they were raped.

Vince took that from me. He took the relationship I was building with my daughter away in one fell swoop. I barely knew my daughter, so it is easy to see how everything went downhill. I was denied the chance to build a relationship with her. Sia looked me in the eye and said she wanted nothing to do with me. She asked me to never contact her and said we would never have a mother-daughter relationship.

Tears in my eyes and my voice thick with emotion, I told Sia I understood why she felt that way but that I wanted her to know what happened. Sia hesitated and I plowed on, explaining I had been the victim and that I hoped she would stand by me.

She couldn't. She didn't know me, and she had just discovered the most shocking family secret. I don't blame Sia for turning her back on me. It is not her fault, and I get why she is angry and upset with me. I am easy to blame, especially since we do not really know each other. Sia does not understand; she barely gave me a chance to explain and discuss it with her.

We have not spoken since then. I have respected her decision and hope that she will contact me one day after she has come to terms with our shared history, shared pain and anguish. I wish we could have had that conversation in almost any other way than how Vince started it. I would have loved to build up our relationship to a point where it could have withstood this blow, to be able to be there for her and heal together. She does not know the hell I went through for her, and it hurts that she wants nothing to do with me.

After Sia found out who her father was, she wanted to meet him. I contacted him and attempted to arrange a meeting, but he refused and said I was lying about him raping me. Angry and needing the truth to be known, I paid for a DNA test. Sia and I both followed through, but her father never did—not even after I sent him the money to have it done.

If there's one thing I wish I could tell my daughter, it is that I am not ashamed to be her mother, and that I understand she is a victim just as much as I am. I had hoped my daughter and I could tell the world that victims of incest don't have to be ashamed. Victims are never at fault for what happened to them. They should not be ashamed of being strong, of being survivors. The people who perpetrate the crimes are those who should be ashamed of their actions.

I think of Sia every day and hope we can build a relationship one day. I long for the opportunity to tell her what I went through when I was pregnant with her. How it felt to have her and then be forced out onto the street with her as an infant. What it was like living in homeless shelters, how I gave up my education for her, the shame I felt every day getting on the school bus with her while we lived in a crack house because I couldn't afford anywhere better. How I paid all of her tuition and educational expenses in Ghana, even when I had nothing for myself, because I knew our family could not pay for her to attend on their own.

The need to tell her these things does not stem from a desire to make her feel guilty or ashamed, but rather to show her how much I love her. To prove that her paternity does not affect how much I care for her. She is my baby girl, my oldest child. Not one inch of this situation is her fault, and I hope she knows that I do not blame her. There is so much I never told her, but I pray that one day we will meet again and that we will both be in a place where we can have an honest, heartfelt talk.

Ultimately, I understand where Sia is coming from, her anger and pain. I do not hold a grudge and never will because my father left when I was two days old and we had a terrible relationship; I hated him and did not even consider him my father for a very long time. My family never supported me and my brother died in the war. If there is one thing I understand, it's feeling abandoned and betrayed.

After the truth came out, Sia moved to North Carolina with family. She is still in touch with Vince and has yet to work through her anger. But she is still a young adult who needs time to work through this, and I accept that. I have not and will not push for contact, but I pray she will reach out to me.

Over the past two years, I have struggled long and hard to forgive Vince for the hurt he has cost me with my eldest child. Even though I knew the truth was going to come out one day, Vince did not give me the opportunity to tell my daughter myself who her father is, or allow me the chance to get my daughter the help we both deserve.

FIFTY-THREE

BY MID-APRIL OF 2014, Vince and I had officially filed for divorce. It was no longer a threat or promise. It had been done. We were still living separately, so it wasn't as hard as it could have been, but it definitely wasn't easy, especially not after my doctor called. She said she had news that might be difficult to hear. I asked if it was okay that I put her on speakerphone so Vince could hear too, and she said it might be best. After I got Vince into the room, we listened as the doctor informed us that Vince had infected me with herpes.

Hearing those words come out of my doctor's mouth was beyond shocking. I had no idea and it was only made worse by the realization Vince was not surprised. I wasn't sure what it meant at the time but resolved myself to figure it out later.

Once we hung up the phone, we sat down and cried together at the news. In that moment, I couldn't sort through my feelings very well. Torn between feeling sorry for myself and feeling sorry for Vince since he was so upset about it, I kept my roller coaster of emotions to myself.

One of the first things he offered was to call off the divorce, but I told him that wasn't realistic. I wanted to be happy and for him to be happy too. No one should stay with anyone out of guilt, and the last thing I wanted was to stay with Vince. Even though staying with him would have been easier, I turned him down.

Fear and anger rolled through me at his suggestion. Knowing that someone I trusted, *my husband*, gave me a virus—made me sick—in a way that cannot be cured made rage boil in my gut. I will live with herpes for the rest of my life. In the future, any man I meet who I want to have a relationship with will have to be told about it.

When I brought this up with Vince, his answer horrified and disgusted me more than what he had done to me. He said that having herpes was my own business, my own secret to share, and that I didn't have to tell anyone—not sexual partners, not even my family. He said that no one in his family knew or would know, that he wasn't going to share this secret with anyone. His confession almost shocked me into silence.

If there's one thing that his family is good at, it is getting into each other's business. They do not keep secrets and always seem to know absolutely everything about each other. Even his forty-year-old daughter knew intimate details about his life that no daughter should know about their father. So the fact that he was not going to tell them, that he was going to take this secret to his grave, showed me nothing more than how disgusted and ashamed he must have felt. Whether that shame and disgust was because he had a sexually transmitted infection, because he infected me, or both, I did not know.

Later on, I realized that he had known about his herpes status and had not told me. That was why he wasn't surprised. I was naïve and stupid to trust him, and his dishonesty led me to be infected with herpes. Then he had the gall to suggest that because of our mutual infection, we might stay together, stay married.

I asked him if what I suspected was true, if he had known when we slept together that he could get me sick too. Shamefaced, he said that he knew that he had it, but that he took medication. He claimed he didn't know that he could give it to me when he didn't have any symptoms. I believed him. I couldn't fault him for knowing next to nothing about herpes; I didn't either.

Vince must have lived in a fantastic fantasy world if he thought that I would want to stay in a marriage of convenience with the very person who had infected me and possibly knowingly exposed me to the virus. I was slowly coming into my own, and thankfully I had enough sense of myself and my worth to know that staying in a relationship without love or even basic respect, if our past was anything to judge by, would be absolutely miserable. I couldn't do it, wouldn't do it. Enough was enough and I wanted out, whether he agreed or not.

● ● ●

Over the next several months, the tension grew between Vince and I, and I no longer felt safe at home. The children and I began to stay at my friends' houses at night. The three of us spent most of the summer in St. Louis with a friend because of how afraid I was of what Vince might do, whether to me or to the kids. He seemed unhinged and had begun drinking. I was worried he was going to hit the children. He had always been somewhat violent with me, but I worried about the moment he turned it on the kids. I worried for both of us—what he would do to them and what I would do to him.

In the late summer, a friend from the time I had owned and run my own store, Tom Christian, sat me down and gave me a much-needed harsh awakening. Tom said, his tone deadly serious and utterly calm, if I stayed with my husband, Vince was going to kill me.

He was right and I knew it. Vince's house was no longer my home—

that much was obvious. Within just a few days, Tom found me a place, rented it in his name because I did not have a job, and helped us move in. Tom and I are good friends to this day, and I will always owe him a debt of gratitude for what he did.

After the children and I moved out, we were brought before the judge, who said that it was my responsibility to make sure Vince picked up Vincetta for his portion of our shared custody agreement. During our early divorce struggles, Vincetta was assigned a law guardian to ensure that her best interests were being addressed. Together with the law guardian and our attorneys, Vince and I agreed to a custody arrangement, and then the judge approved it.

The custody arrangement had been an entire ordeal in and of itself, but I had never been more thankful of having filed numerous police reports against Vince than I was when they were used as evidence against Vince maintaining full custody of our daughter. Over the years, abuse reports and various domestic disturbance reports had been filed by both of us, but just after the children and I moved out, Vince tried to run me over.

I was standing in the driveway in the middle of the day when he floored it and attempted to run me into the garage door. Immediately after it happened, I called the police and reported what happened. There were several neighborhood witnesses and even tire marks on the driveway, but the cops decided against arresting him because Vince claimed he thought he was in reverse and that it was an accident.

It wasn't.

Not that it mattered to the Lake Ozark Police Department. Either way, that report went on file and it saved me from possibly losing my other daughter to Vince too. That report, the numerous others from previous years, and my medical records that showed the history of abuse were used to deny Vince the sole custody he sought. Instead, my children would live with me and Vince would have visitation every other weekend provided he was not using drugs or alcohol.

When custody was first being argued, Child Protective Services came to evaluate our home and how the children interacted with both Vince and I. While some people find this very invasive, I was pleased to find out that the children had not been harmed or hurt by our vicious arguments over the years. That despite everything they had heard us say and how Vince had been treating me, the children were resilient and unafraid of him. After all, he never did anything to hurt them.

As much as I worried about it, Vince never once hurt the children. He never made Abraham feel any less his child than Vincetta is. To this day, Abraham considers Vince his father. Vince, too, seems to consider Abraham his son. Every visitation weekend, Vince takes both children rather than just Vincetta. Though he does not pay child support for Abraham, Vince never hesitates to give birthday and holiday gifts to Abraham, and Abraham has never indicated that he feels unloved or unwelcome in Vince's house.

● ● ●

After the divorce was finalized, Vince and I took a little while before we really started talking again. By late 2015, the divorce was settled and it was over. My life went back to being relatively quiet. There was no more fighting with Vince or worrying about my health and safety to occupy my time. All of a sudden, it was only my kids and me. I only had to deal with my ex-husband every other weekend.

After several months of this, Vince and I started talking again. It was not long after Vincetta, Abraham, and I moved into a new place, after we made ourselves a home, that Vince and I fell back into old habits. My forgiving nature and the promise of good sex lured me back into Vince's bed. We became on-again, off-again, but were not really together either.

Even now, I am not sure what we were, and I didn't know then either. At one point, I asked him what we were, what he wanted us to be. He did not have a straightforward answer any more than I did.

Our mutual confusion made up my mind once I considered how unfair our relationship was to the kids. They did not deserve to be stuck in the middle of our will-they-won't-they relationship. But beyond the children's feelings, the connection between Vince and I didn't feel right either. Something just felt off, and I knew we had to stop. I told him as much, and he agreed. So we started dating other people.

Up until that point, Vince had been supporting the children and me, but he has stepped back other than the required child support. I am supporting my family now. While being the breadwinner can be stressful at times, it is also very rewarding. I have always enjoyed and taken pride in being self-sufficient, and now is no different. As of the writing of this book, Vince and I are good friends, but nothing more. I trust him to care for the children on his weekends, and he trusts me to look after them the rest of the time. I do not know what the future holds, but I do know that we made the right choice—both in ending things and in getting a divorce.

FIFTY-FOUR

THE ONLY THING THAT changed my life more than school was my divorce. When it came to school, I did not even have a GED, let alone a high school diploma. Yet I still somehow managed to get into three different colleges and cosmetology school.

The first school that accepted me, Lincoln University, had me take a series of entrance exams to determine my ability, since I was an immigrant without a GED or diploma. After I passed, they allowed me to sign up for classes. Setting foot on campus and walking through the classroom doors were the most empowering things I had ever done up until that point. Throughout all of my classes and years in school, despite the regular upheaval of my life, I did fairly well in my classes and studied hard to make it that way.

Being more of a hands-on learner, I did struggle somewhat with retaining information I had only read and did not have a practical application for, but I muddled through, motivated by the sense of self-esteem I received from just being a higher education student, of having achieved that when no one ever thought I would be capable of it. Going to college was the first time I had ever mingled with people who had standards, who were not just content with their lot in life, who wanted to make something of themselves for whatever reason. It was my first opportunity to see how people with privilege lived.

Even just passing those first entrance exams sent my self-esteem rocketing into the stratosphere. I had watched my youngest sister climb the ladder, seeking better things for herself, and all I wanted was the opportunities she had: the chance to prove to myself and everyone else that I was someone smart and capable, that I was worth more than they could ever know, that I could be better than the hand I was dealt. This drive is what led me to begin to take GED classes before I even thought to just apply to a local university.

● ● ●

In the same ways that school changed my life and completely altered my perception of myself, so did my marriage to and then my divorce from Vince. Our relationship had been so rocky and full of ups and downs that I never really knew where I stood. I was constantly just trying to get my bearings and stay on my feet. In both positive and negative ways, Vince had always had the ability to completely throw me for a loop.

Our relationship had many problems, and many were evident from day one, though they did not truly make themselves known until later. After we were married, Vince tried to make me into the perfect piece of arm candy, an exotic trophy wife. Despite the massive boost in self-esteem from attending school and starting to figure out who I was, I was still insecure and unsure of myself and my place in the world. So when Vince wanted me to change things about myself for him, I did not really hesitate to accept and I did not put up much of a fight. Sometimes it was because I was afraid of him, and other times I did not want to fight or did not know I should.

Vince heavily encouraged my body issues, whether he meant to purposefully or not. If I gained even a little bit of weight, he would complain that he could not feel my ribs when we laid in bed, which was more than hypocritical of him, given his own physique. But being thin generally means having a small chest, which Vince was not happy about, so he made me get breast implants. Similarly, he found tattoos attractive and had me get one on my back, and he paid to have thousands of dollars of work done on my teeth, which is one thing I am grateful for because healthy teeth are very important.

Vince was controlling. He dictated the food I ate, the restaurants we went to, and the stores I shopped at. He was even particular about the way I spoke and would criticize me if I sounded too black. I found this particularly frustrating given how rude and embarrassing he could be. Vince had a tendency to be incredibly rude to service workers, as if they were beneath him, a particular point of view I have never understood. My grandmother raised me to respect everyone, and I hope that I will pass that belief on to my children.

Even though there was all of that negativity surrounding us, he changed my life. If Vince and I had never met, I never would have learned so much about myself. At first, it felt like I was Cinderella and he was my prince. We fell in love and it was beautiful. The pain and bitterness came later, but he showed me love and taught me how to love. It was not love at first sight; I didn't know how to love before I met him. My heart was surrounded in darkness, and Vince is the one who broke through and shined the light that brought me back to the world. He showed me kindness and care; he spoiled me and doted on me.

There were definitely many things wrong with our relationship, and I know it was not a particularly healthy one, but I also know that most men would not do as much for me as Vince did. They would not have opened a store for me, to give me a sense of purpose and responsibility. They would not have bothered to teach me to love myself, to be proud of myself and my accomplishments, to show the world my hard-earned strength after everything that I have been through. Vince did, and I will always love him for that.

Meeting Vince sent my life in a completely different direction than it otherwise would have gone. The moment we locked eyes outside that gas station, my life turned abruptly around and took a different path than the one I had been set on. But the most valuable thing Vince ever gave me was the knowledge that I shouldn't settle for anything less than what I deserve. Learning that is what allowed me to become someone who helps her family instead of needing help.

FIFTY-FIVE

AFTER OUR DIVORCE WAS FINALIZED, many things immediately changed. Even though he did help us initially with finances, I went from being fairly well off and wanting for nothing to making it work. It was a difficult adjustment, but I've kept my head up. My kids and I have a good life. We aren't struggling to make ends meet, but we aren't in a position to hire a housekeeper either. I drive a good, reliable car. Our house is nice and well kept, and we are happily living in the middle. I'm in no way ungrateful for what I have; I just acknowledge that initially, it felt like a big step down from my previous economic status.

Right now, I'm exactly where I need to be. I'm working on figuring out what I want, how I can live a life that helps and inspires people. I want to work with people to make their lives better. I'm currently working as a personal trainer and a certified nurse's aid, but I would like to go back to school and actually finish my degree. I want to figure out how I can best use my talents.

While writing this chapter of the book, I accomplished one of the goals

I had set for myself. I had a tubal ligation. Much like both my mother and my father, all of my children have different fathers. As I do not want any more children and because I do not want to perpetuate what I see as an irresponsible cycle, I found a doctor who was willing to tie my tubes. Some women, depending on their age, race, and numerous other factors, can have a difficult time finding a doctor willing to do this if they are younger than thirty-five. I was blessed to have been of an age and to find a practice where I was not questioned too unreasonably about my decision.

Now that I can be assured of not having any more children, I feel like I have taken a serious step in controlling my own life and destiny. I am free to make my own choices and pursue my dreams without having to worry about providing for yet another child, no matter how much I would love them.

With the publication of this book on the horizon, I am pleased to say that another one of my big goals for my post-divorce life is nearly achieved. I can only hope that by sharing my story, others will see what I have been through and understand that there is light at the end of the tunnel. That there are things that you can do to change where you are now, that you can make the best of a rotten situation. There is nothing that cannot be overcome with enough dedication, perseverance, and will. Even if a problem in your life seems insurmountable, you only have to be creative to solve it. There is no shame in asking for help, either. It is always better to ask than to wish you had later.

EPILOGUE

"WITH GOD, ALL THINGS ARE POSSIBLE."
—Matthew 19:26

There is nothing that cannot be overcome. I believe that we do not encounter challenges in our lives that we cannot handle. Whether, like me, you attribute this to God, or to the universe and chance does not matter. All that matters is perseverance, strength, and the willingness to ask for and accept help when needed. With those three things, human beings can survive. We may be flesh and bone, but we are not fragile. The trials and tragedies and terrors we face in our lives are horrible, traumatic, and may make us desperate, but all of it is temporary. Sometimes, the only thought that could get me through the day was knowing that the sun would rise again tomorrow, that the day would end and I could try again.

After my divorce, I turned inward and focused on healing myself, bettering myself, and pushing myself to be a better mother, better woman, and better Christian. One of the first things I did on my journey was to push away negative people in my life, people who never brought me joy, and people who only seemed to want me around to show off how much better they were in their eyes.

With the support of my sister, Bendu, I no longer speak with my mother's side of the family for this very reason. I know where I came from and who I am, and I am content with this. I do not need to hear my aunties' and cousins' negative opinions of me. I do not need to prove myself to them. Similarly, of my father's children, the only one I still have a relationship with, the only one I still really consider family, is my little brother Ceephas. Since letting go of the notion that I needed to maintain contact with my family in order to be happy, I have been much more content with my life. Without their constant negative presence, I have been able to heal and grow, to seek out healthy ways of living without being bombarded by manipulative and cruel commentary.

This opened up numerous doors for me. I was able to really explore what I value, why, and how I got to where I was. In learning about myself, I discovered so much more of the world and my place within it. God put me on this earth to help people free themselves of their chains, to teach them how to fight the battle. This is why I have written this book. This is why I have put myself and my story of abandonment, abuse, incest, and violence into the public eye.

My goal is to show victims of abuse, of rape, of incest that they are not at fault. That what happened to them is entirely the fault of their abuser. There is no place for shame in being a survivor. There is shame in hurting people. There is shame in being the abuser, not the abused. This knowledge was not easily gained, and even after I understood it intellectually, it took a long time before I could believe it emotionally. Between self-loathing and low self-esteem, I fought myself every step of the way. For every step I took toward understanding, I would have to overcome a mountain of guilt, shame, and desperation. There are still days that I struggle, but they are few and far between now. Every day gets easier, and every person I can help helps me too. By reaching out and touching people's lives, I can only hope to trigger larger, more systemic change.

One of the first people I helped was a young woman called Ricki. Ricki and I met at a club, and I soon noticed a pattern in her behavior. She would go out, get drunk, sleep around with whoever took her home, and then feel deeply shamed and guilty in the morning. She was looking for love and attention but didn't know how to go about it in a way that didn't hurt her. While some people may find this pattern of behavior perfectly acceptable, it upset her and made her already low self-esteem even lower. She felt like she needed to get drunk in order to get the attention.

At first, I thought she just liked to party, but after a few months of knowing her, I could see how every man she slept with seemed to eat away at her, how much she regretted doing what she did, even though she had been consenting at the time. The turning point for her was when we went out together one evening and she wound up back at some guy's house. We had met two men, friends, who wanted to hook up. I was not interested, but Ricki really wanted to go back to their place. Since I wasn't about to leave her alone with two strange men, I went along.

When we got there, we had another drink, and Ricki started to lose her inhibitions. When I asked her if she wanted to go home, she insisted that she wanted to go upstairs with one of the men. She was an adult, and she wasn't slurring her words, losing track of the conversation, stumbling around, or any other sign of being more than a bit tipsy. Despite her clarity, I tried to get her to come home with me and sleep it off, but she refused and pushed me away, leading the man upstairs. I sat on the sofa and waited for her.

The next morning on the way home, she asked me to help her stop drinking and learn to make better choices. Together, we worked to raise her self-esteem by empowering her and learning about self-confidence, consent, choices, and healthy attitudes toward sex and relationships. She built a new foundation for herself, and I am so proud of whatever part I played in helping her to love and respect herself.

To this day, Ricki has not touched a drop of alcohol. Whenever someone asks how she did it, she says that I was the messenger God sent to help her. I can only hope to live up to that high praise.

Ricki reminded me of myself and the struggles that I have overcome on my path to self-acceptance, love, and confidence. Even after all of the tragedy I have faced, I learned that there is still hope and love in this world. I just had to allow myself to see it, to take a chance that some of that happiness might belong to me. Furthermore, confidence taught me something my son Abraham was born with: the ability to put aside hate and anger and simply walk away.

As we come to the end of my story, there are people I would like to thank. People who, if they had not been in my life, I would not be able to be where I am today. I would not be the person I am today. I may not have had the strength to pull through and push myself toward success. These are people I believe God brought into my life. They have given me shelter in the storm, shoulders to lean on, and strength when my own was long gone.

First and foremost, I need to thank my son, Abraham. I love all my children, and wish all of them happy, healthy lives, but God truly blessed me with Abraham. Never before have I met such a kind, sweet, thoughtful, and caring child with such an innate sense of morality. At school, everyone from his principal to the janitor has told me what a generous and gentle soul he is. My past made me into an angry, hateful person for much of my life, something I have strived to overcome. I have worked hard to make sure I do not antagonize and start problems, but I have never been someone who can turn the other cheek. Abraham can and does, and I envy his ability to be the better person even when wronged.

When my little boy was in first grade, he came home from school with a note from his teacher. I read it and rage filled me, but I kept calm and asked him what happened. Much like the note said, Abraham explained that he was out on the playground and one of the boys tried to start a fight with him. Abraham attempted to remove himself from the situation, but it escalated to pushing and soon the other boy kicked him in the crotch.

Abraham never tried to retaliate, the note was quick to tell me. I told Abraham that did the right thing by trying to get away, but that it is okay to use enough force to defend yourself.

"No," Abraham insisted, "it's not nice, Mommy. I won't hurt anyone."

I was shocked, simply stunned at this deeply pacifist belief that Abraham has, a belief that I have never believed or followed myself. He has often been teased for being calm, being a peacemaker and a mama's boy. He refuses to push back, to engage with his bullies. Instead, he has learned to get away, to run and go to a teacher. To ignore bullies because he absolutely believes that turning to violence is the wrong answer. While I may not practice this myself, I am happy to have such a gentle-natured son.

Abraham is more than kind and sweet, though. He is nurturing and caring. If at any time I feel sick or sad or upset, Abraham is at my side, asking if there is anything he can do to help. I worry that he tries to take on too much, that he cares too much, in his looking after me and his little sister, but he is who he is. I do not allow myself to put my burdens on him, but I also won't force him to go out and play if he would rather stay inside and sit with me if I am having a bad day.

While Vince and I were going through our divorce, my bad days were more frequent, and each and every time I was upset, even if I tried to hide it, he knew. He knew, and he would ask if I was okay and if I needed anything. No matter how hard I tried to get him to go out and play, he would sit and cuddle into my side, telling me he loved me, that I was strong, and that it would all be okay. As he comforted me, I worried that it was too much for him, that I was hurting him by being sad. But even when I tried to hide my feelings from him, my sensitive little boy knew and would stay by me until I felt better.

Abraham might be a child, but he is very aware of his family. He wants us to be happy and will do anything he can to make it so. When money was tight and I was struggling to put food on the table, Abraham dumped his piggybank onto his bed and offered me his change without my ever having even thought about asking. He just offered it with a sad but hopeful little smile, saying, "Can this buy some bread, Mommy?"

I wouldn't be where I am without my son. I would not have his sweet, honest, and loyal presence in my life reminding me that there is more to this world than greed, anger, and hate. Abraham truly is God's gift to me, and I thank both my son and God for him every day.

I would also like to thank my sister Bendu and her husband, Faheem. While Bendu and I do not actually share DNA, we were raised together in my grandmother's home. While at the compound, we were pregnant at the same time as teenagers. This jump-started our bond, and we grew closer. Now that we are adults, we have been through hell and back together and understand each other in the way that usually only siblings can due to shared experiences.

If there is anyone that Abraham takes after regarding his temperament, it is Bendu. She is so sweet and kind; she is the kind of person who looks after everyone else before even thinking of herself. She would give a stranger on the street the shirt off her back if they needed it. Much like I do with Abraham, I worried about her for years because of how easily she is taken advantage of simply because of her nature. I worried until she met Faheem after moving to the United States.

Together, they live in Chicago with their three children. When they met, Bendu was still in nursing school and Faheem was in the military. Now she is a nurse, gainfully employed at a local hospital, and he is a community activist who seeks to promote equality and better lives and opportunities for black Americans. Without their influence, their words of encouragement, empowerment, and strength, I would not be where I am today. Both my sister and her husband have stood by me through the divorce and every trouble that I have encountered. Where some people are put off by my blunt and honest attitude, both Bendu and Faheem appreciate it. Bendu because she knows that I do not have a hidden agenda, and Faheem because he is much the same way.

Faheem's love and support of my sister has shown me what a good man looks like. He supports his family like a rock and ensures they survive whatever is thrown at them. Even though one of my sister's children is not Faheem's biologically, he has never shown anything but equal and unconditional love for all three. Their relationship and the life they have created for each other inspires me. One day, I would like to have a relationship as happy and healthy as theirs, but it is not my focus right now. I am intent on bettering the lives of my children and myself first, before seeking out a partner.

I am ever thankful for the support and loyalty Bendu and Faheem have shown me and my children. There are not words to explain how much it has meant or how much good it has done for me.

Finally, I would like to thank Tom Christian, who has done so much for me and my children. This man has gone above and beyond the call of a friend. He stood by me through thick and thin and was always there when I needed him. Tom is a loyal, passionate man who has never made me feel bad for how much I have leaned on him. Tom gave up so much for me, and I am eternally grateful.

My own battle was long and hard fought, but I have found a purpose in life: supporting survivors of abuse—emotional, sexual, physical—and teaching them how to help themselves heal, to empower them to make changes in their lives for the better by promoting self-confidence. We are survivors, and we need to help each other understand the strength inherent in survival and how to use that strength to rebuild our self-confidence and to help us in our healing. While it may still be a difficult journey, self-confidence helps to stop people from making choices that might be detrimental to themselves. It allows for the ability to walk away rather than stay because we think we deserve their negativity.

CHARLESETTA KOLB was born in Liberia in 1981. The daughter of an abusive mother and an absentee father who left behind in Africa when he immigrated to the United States, Charlesetta has been a fighter her entire life. Caught up in Liberia's coup d'etat, Charlesetta was forced to the extremes in order to survive. Without family support, she lived among the rebels and was forced to serve as a soldier. After returning to her family, Charlesetta was raped by her half brother and became pregnant.

Through trial, struggle, and hardship, Charlesetta has fought for herself and her children. Now living in Missouri, she hopes to serve as inspiration for others who are struggling. This is her first book.

Made in the USA
Monee, IL
27 March 2022

93625791R00105